WORLD WAR II

BY
GEORGE LEE

COPYRIGHT © 1995 Mark Twain Media, Inc.

Printing No. CD–1835

Mark Twain Media, Inc., Publishers
Distributed by Carson-Dellosa Publishing Company, Inc.

TABLE OF CONTENTS

INTRODUCTION

All around the world, travel poster signs were going up; in the United States Uncle Sam pointed his finger at men and told them "I want **YOU** for the Army." In case they failed to notice that invitation, another came that began with the word: "Greetings." That was long ago, and the men who accepted this warm invitation are now the grandfathers and great-grandfathers of today's school children. Stories that men tried to erase from their minds after the war are now family legends. These men served with pride and honor and do not want their posterity to forget what their nation meant to them.

World War II was what one writer called "The Good War." There were genuine bad guys who, with diabolical evil, planned the extermination of the "subhuman" races. These bad guys were so evil that those fighting them felt no sacrifice was too great. The men who fought for those bad guys were not always bad guys themselves. They had been subjected to brainwashing that twisted racism into national pride, injustice into just punishment, and atrocities into the unfortunate consequences of war.

A book this size cannot include everything that happened between 1939 and 1945. This is only an attempt to sketch what happened and why. Hopefully, family narratives will fill in the gaps for students with the anecdotes that cannot be told here.

The material in this book is not easy, and some portions may not fit every student's maturity level, but the parts dealing with the Holocaust and the cruel treatment of conquered peoples must be included so more mature students can understand what the war was about.

—THE AUTHOR—

Time Line of World War II Events

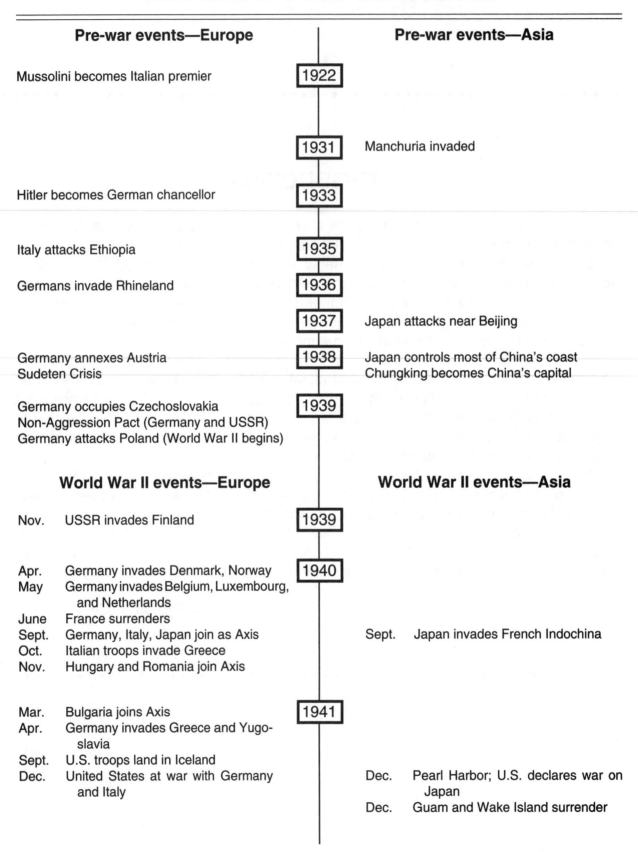

Pre-war events—Europe		Pre-war events—Asia
Mussolini becomes Italian premier	**1922**	
	1931	Manchuria invaded
Hitler becomes German chancellor	**1933**	
Italy attacks Ethiopia	**1935**	
Germans invade Rhineland	**1936**	
	1937	Japan attacks near Beijing
Germany annexes Austria Sudeten Crisis	**1938**	Japan controls most of China's coast Chungking becomes China's capital
Germany occupies Czechoslovakia Non-Aggression Pact (Germany and USSR) Germany attacks Poland (World War II begins)	**1939**	

World War II events—Europe / World War II events—Asia

	World War II events—Europe		World War II events—Asia	
Nov.	USSR invades Finland	**1939**		
Apr.	Germany invades Denmark, Norway	**1940**		
May	Germany invades Belgium, Luxembourg, and Netherlands			
June	France surrenders			
Sept.	Germany, Italy, Japan join as Axis		Sept.	Japan invades French Indochina
Oct.	Italian troops invade Greece			
Nov.	Hungary and Romania join Axis			
Mar.	Bulgaria joins Axis	**1941**		
Apr.	Germany invades Greece and Yugo-slavia			
Sept.	U.S. troops land in Iceland			
Dec.	United States at war with Germany and Italy		Dec.	Pearl Harbor; U.S. declares war on Japan
			Dec.	Guam and Wake Island surrender

World War II events—Europe (cont.) | World War II events—Asia (cont.)

	1942	Jan. — Manila falls
		Jan. — Japan invades Dutch East Indies
		Feb. — Singapore falls
		Apr. — Bataan surrenders to Japan
		Apr. — Doolittle air raid on Tokyo
		May — Battle of Coral Sea
		May — Corregidor surrenders to Japan
June — Germany invades Russia		June — Battle of Midway
July — Germans capture Tobruk, N. Africa		
		Aug. — U.S. marines on Guadalcanal
Sept. — German troops enter Stalingrad		
Oct. — British attack at El Alamein		
Nov. — Allies land in North Africa		
Nov. — British capture Tobruk		
Nov. — Russian offensive at Stalingrad		
Feb. — Germans surrender at Stalingrad	**1943**	
Mar. — Afrika Korps surrenders		
		May — Battle of Bismarck Sea
July — Allies invade Sicily		
Nov. — Russians recapture Kiev		Nov. — U.S. invasions of Bougainville and Tarawa
Nov. — Cairo Conference		
Jan. — Siege of Leningrad broken	**1944**	Jan. — United States attacks Kwajalein
June — Landing at Normandy		June — United States invades Saipan
June — V–1 attacks on London.		June — B–29s attack Tokyo
		July — United States invades Guam
Aug. — Allied troops land in southern France		
		Oct. — United States invades Leyte, Battle of Leyte Gulf
Dec. — Battle of Bulge begins and is stopped		
Jan. — Russians reach Warsaw	**1945**	Jan. — Allies invade Luzon
		Feb. — United States invades Iwo Jima
Apr. — Russians in Vienna and Berlin suburbs		Apr. — United States invades Okinawa
May — Hitler commits suicide; Berlin surrenders		
May — VE-Day ends war with Germany		
July — Potsdam Conference		
		Aug. — Atomic bombs on Hiroshima and Nagasaki
		Aug. — Japan agrees to surrender
		Aug. — VJ-Day ends war with Japan

THE LEGACY OF VERSAILLES

As a boy Woodrow Wilson witnessed the devastation that left the South in ruins after the Civil War. Three years after World War I began in Europe, after much soul searching, President Wilson asked Congress to declare war. Sending men to die in a war on foreign soil had to have some noble purpose, and Wilson justified (to himself as much as to Congress) his call to arms by saying that the "world must be made safe for democracy."

The American "doughboy" who was part of the American Expeditionary Force (AEF) responded to that challenge and, singing "It's a

Britain's Lloyd George, Italy's Orlando, France's Clemenceau, and U.S. President Wilson met in Versailles to negotiate peace.

Long Way to Tipperary," went off to France. He fought well at Chateau Thierry, Belleau Wood, and in the Meuse-Argonne campaign in a war that featured frightening new weapons: submarines, airplanes, machine guns, and poison gas. Like his grandfather who had fought in the Civil War, he heard the artillery shells, the screams of the wounded, and the terror of hand-to-hand combat. Then the Kaiser abdicated (surrendered the throne), and the Germans signed an armistice on November 11, 1918. The doughboys came marching home.

President Wilson wanted to fulfill his promises in person. He wanted to make sure this was "the war to end all wars" and to make the "world safe for democracy." During the war he drafted his solution for international problems, the Fourteen Points. Included were proposals for freedom of the seas, arms reduction, boundary adjustments so people could live with others of the same nationality, and a "general association of nations" to protect the boundaries and political independence of all nations.

Wilson traveled to Versailles where he met English Prime Minister David Lloyd George and France's Premier Georges Clemenceau for the first time. Unlike Wilson, Clemenceau (nicknamed the Tiger) had no illusions about world peace. He predicted another war within 20 years. Lloyd George, England's prime minister since 1916, had built his career on following his own instincts. He sided with neither the idealistic Wilson nor the fatalist Clemenceau. As they sat at the table and hammered out policies, they were determining the fate of the world.

History would not look kindly on some of the decisions that were made at Versailles, and the failures of world leaders in 1919–1920 were painfully obvious to those who saw the results 20 years later. A brief list of failures follows.

1. Germany was defeated but not conquered. The victors reduced its army and navy to shadows of their former sizes. The Allies required reparations (the penalty for losing a war). They took away the region of Alsace-Lorraine and gave it to France permanently. The Saar Basin was placed in French hands for 15 years. Poland was given a strip of West Prussia (the Polish Corridor). Germany's overseas empire was divided among England, France, Japan, New Zealand, Australia, Belgium, and South Africa. They did away with the monarchy and forced Germany to form the feeble Weimar Republic. The "War Guilt" clause saddled Germany with the responsibility for causing the war.

    Germany had not been a battleground, so even though it lost its colonies and some of its most valuable territory, resources, and population, Germany still had the large population and industrial base needed to regain power in a few years. A German recovery posed a threat to its neighbors.

2. All of Austria, Hungary, and Czechoslovakia and parts of Poland, Romania, Yugoslavia, and northern Italy were carved out of the old Austro-Hungarian Empire. Austria, in a separate 1919 treaty (Treaty of St. Germain) was forbidden to ever become part of Germany *(Anschluss).* Austria was kept alive by foreign loans, and Hungary by selling its bonds in other countries. These small, vulnerable nations were tempting to large and greedy neighbors.

3. Russia, still going through a revolution, was not invited to the peace talks. There were reasons, of course: their withdrawal from the war; the Treaty of Brest-Litovsk, which freed Germany to concentrate all of its forces on the western front; and most compelling of all, the fact that Communists had seized power in Russia and their talk of world revolution made them outcasts.

4. The League of Nations was toothless when its rulings were ignored by larger countries. Article X of the League covenant (constitution) called for members to protect one another against external aggression. Article XII required that members settle disputes through arbitration or a judicial tribunal and refrain from war for at least three months. Article XVI was an agreement to use economic and financial boycotts against any nation not abiding by the covenant. If the violator were a weak nation, the League might control it, but what if it were Germany or Japan? The U.S. Senate's rejection of the Treaty of Versailles damaged League prestige, but the lack of support for League principles by the large nations left the League totally ineffective when powerful nations defied it.

Debate

The peace terms at Versailles were unfair to Germany.

Name_____ Date _____

POINTS TO CONSIDER

1. Why did American opponents of the League of Nations concentrate on Article X?

_____

_____

_____

_____

_____

2. What parts of the Fourteen Points do you think would be most important (and least important) in preventing wars?

_____

_____

_____

_____

_____

3. If you were German, how would you feel about the War Guilt clause?

_____

_____

_____

_____

_____

Name _____ Date _____

CHALLENGES

1. What were two short statements reflecting Wilson's goals in World War I?

_____

_____

2. What were four World War I weapons never before used to any large extent in a major war?

_____

_____

3. What list included Wilson's ideas for preventing another war?

_____

4. Who represented France and England at Versailles?

_____

5. What region did Germany lose to France permanently? What region did it lose for 15 years?

_____

6. What was the new German government called?

_____

7. What new nations were completely composed of territory that had been the Austro-Hungarian Empire?

_____

_____

8. What was Austria forbidden to do by the Treaty of St. Germain?

_____

9. What did Article X of the League covenant provide?

_____

_____

10. What did Article XVI provide?

_____

_____

THE RISE OF DICTATORS

When wars end, democracies rush to dismantle their military might. The citizen soldier wants to rejoin the civilians, and taxpaying voters want the military forces reduced. After World War I, nations tried to defend themselves by signing agreements. The Washington Naval Conference (1921–1922) limited the number of aircraft carriers and capital ships by setting a ratio of 5:5:3:1.67:1.67 on the navies of the United States, Great Britain, Japan, France, and Italy. The Locarno Treaties (1925) set the boundaries of Germany, Belgium, and France, and allowed Germany's entry into the League of Nations. The Kellogg-Briand Pact was signed by 62 nations and discarded war as a national policy. At the London Naval Conference (1930) members agreed to postpone building new capital ships until 1936, but a signing nation could increase its navy if it felt its national security was endangered.

Fascist leaders Adolf Hitler (left) and Benito Mussolini (right) joined forces in 1936.

While others saw a rosy picture ahead because of these agreements, Winston Churchill saw future dangers. In 1928 he predicted that future wars would involve whole populations, and with their very existence at stake, nations would use whatever means they had to win the war. He wrote: "Death stands at attention, obedient, expectant, ready to serve, ready to shear away the peoples en masse; ready, if called on, to pulverise, without hope of repair, what is left of civilisation." Adding to the weapons and the total nature of modern war was the rise to power of the dictators. If monarchy and republican government had had their day, it appeared in the 1930s that dictatorship was the rising star in the world. Dictators think and act differently from presidents or prime ministers who are limited by legislatures and courts. In dictatorships: (1) all power is in the hands of one person or a small elite group; (2) no law or court prevents them from doing as they wish; (3) citizens' rights may be taken away at any time; (4) terror is a common tool to force obedience; and (5) dictators often mislead themselves and their nation with dreams of national glory through military expansion.

In *RUSSIA* Vladimir Lenin's Communist Party came to power in 1917, created a new secret police *(Cheka),* and either killed, imprisoned, or exiled any opponent. While civil war raged in Russia, the *Comintern* (Communist International Party) spread propaganda to other nations. After suffering a stroke in 1922, Lenin's health declined, and a power struggle between Josef Stalin and Leon Trotsky began. Stalin won and Trotsky was exiled.

JAPAN was given its first constitution in 1890 by the emperor. It created the Diet (legislature) with limited powers and gave rights to the people (removable at any time "according to the law"). Japan found two roads to success in the twentieth century. One was through the <u>military</u>. In 1894–1895 Japan easily defeated the Chinese in the Sino-Japanese War, and its troops had joined others to crush China's Boxer Rebellion in 1900. A surprise attack on the Russian fleet opened the Russo-Japanese War (1904–1905). Despite naval

5

and battlefield victories, Japan had to agree to disappointing peace terms drawn up by U.S. president Theodore Roosevelt. In 1910 Japan annexed Korea. In World War I Japan took the German leasehold at Kiaochow. Japanese militarists saw colonialism in East Asia as the way to national glory and prosperity.

Japanese <u>industry and trade</u> also grew tremendously in the early twentieth century. The visit of 16 U.S. battleships in 1908 convinced Japan of the need to expand its navy. Once it saw the need to catch up with the Western world, Japan quickly progressed. In 1872 it had its first railroad; by 1914 Japan had 6,000 miles of track. In 1899 Japan had no iron ships; by 1914 the Japanese merchant marine was larger than the French fleet. The business community saw trade as the way to meet the needs of Japan's rapidly growing population. The Depression seriously weakened the influence of business, however. In 1932 the liberal premier was assassinated, and Admiral Saito replaced him. The militarists had won; the struggle between the military and business was over.

ITALY left World War I with a nearly bankrupt government, little industry, high unemployment, and a lack of food for its 40 million people. Political divisions made it impossible for any leader to stay in office long enough to accomplish anything. In the streets, gangs of Socialist hoodlums battled the Fascists' thugs. Fascist leader Benito Mussolini had once been a Socialist, but left the party in 1915 when he supported the war and the party didn't. Mussolini fought in the war as an enlisted man. When it ended, he formed the Fascist (from *fascio,* meaning "a club") Party. Known as Black Shirts, Fascist squads followed all orders from Mussolini. To industrialists and many common citizens, Fascists seemed to be the only alternative to a Communist takeover.

In an October 1922 speech in Naples, Mussolini said that "either the government will be given to us or we will march on Rome." His Black Shirts marched on Rome, the army did not interfere, and King Victor Emmanuel III timidly asked Mussolini to form a cabinet.

Fascism had a clear philosophy. It glorified the state (government), and the leaders of that state ran the nation's economy and society. Any criticism or opposition to *Il Duce* (The Leader) was treason, and when Socialist deputy Giacomo Matteotti charged the Fascists with corruption, he was murdered. After 1928 only the names of Fascist candidates appeared on ballots; voters had the choice of voting "yes" or "no" on them. Meanwhile, Mussolini's philosophy and style were observed and admired by Adolf Hitler.

Debate

Nations that are reasonably prosperous and peaceful are not likely to choose dictatorship.

Name _____ Date _____

POINTS TO CONSIDER

1. Do you think the agreements made after World War I gave the democracies a false sense of security?

_____

_____

_____

_____

_____

2. Why do nations sometimes prefer dictators over freedom?

_____

_____

_____

_____

_____

3. If you had lived in Japan during the 1920s, how would you have answered those who felt that military expansion was better for Japan than trade?

_____

_____

_____

_____

_____

Name_____ Date _____

CHALLENGES

1. What types of ships were limited by the Washington Naval Conference?

_____

2. What was the purpose of the Kellogg-Briand Pact?

_____

_____

3. What two qualities of modern wars bothered Churchill?

_____

_____

4. How is dictatorship defined?

_____

_____

_____

5. Which of Lenin's agencies spread communism to other nations?

_____

6. What nations did Japan either fight or annex between 1894 and 1915?

_____

_____

7. When did the militarists take over the civilian government of Japan?

_____

8. Whom did the Fascists battle in the streets of Italy?

_____

9. Who were the Black Shirts?

_____

10. What lesson did Giacomo Matteotti's death teach?

_____

_____

8

NAZI GERMANY

When the Kaiser was chased out of Germany in November 1918, a provisional government led by the Social Democrats took over. This party was divided into many factions. The Spartacists were the most radical group, similar to the Russian Bolsheviks (Communists). The Spartacists' 1919 effort to overthrow the provisional government was crushed by the army.

At Weimar in February 1919, Germans drew up a democratic constitution. The president and *Reichstag* (lower house) were elected with parties represented in proportion to party strength in the election (a party with 30 percent of the votes got 30 percent of the seats). The chancellor (prime minister) was responsible to the president and Reichstag. Each German state sent delegates to the upper house, the *Reichsrat.*

The new republic was threatened by Communists on the left and Nationalists on the right. The political right wanted to reestablish the old undemocratic system. A Nationalist plot, the Kapp Putsch (uprising), took over Berlin for a time in 1920, but the Socialist workers cut off

Adolf Hitler

public utilities and the ringleaders fled. Then in 1923 came another putsch led by a young fanatic, Adolf Hitler.

Born in Austria in 1889, Hitler was the product of an unhappy childhood and a frustrated effort to become an artist. Reduced to painting postcards before World War I, he eagerly joined the German army when the opportunity came. He was rewarded with a corporal's rank, an Iron Cross medal, and a wound at the Battle of the Somme. After recovering, he drifted to Munich where he often attended meetings of revolutionaries in the dark beer halls. In June 1919 he joined the National Socialist (Nazi) Party as member No. 7. This group hated Jews, the Treaty of Versailles, the Communists, and the democratic Weimar Republic.

Hitler was an expert organizer, and under his leadership, the Nazi Party grew quickly, picking up dreamers, hoodlums, and misfits as members. He developed the party flag with its swastika and the party slogan: "Germany awake!" From Italy's Fascists he borrowed the Roman salute, the pageantry, images of the heroic past, and the idea of special uniforms. Hitler said: "People need a good scare. They want someone to be afraid of." The Nazi's SA, the Brown Shirts, provided that fear. They battled socialists, marched in noisy parades, intimidated any critics, and lived by the slogan: "We're brawling our way to greatness."

In 1923, in defiance of an ordinance against demonstrations, Hitler led a march to capture control of Munich (the Beer Garden Putsch). Trapped by the police in a narrow street, the Nazis surrendered. Hitler was sentenced to five years in prison. His friend Hermann Göring was wounded.

While he was in prison, Hitler wrote *Mein Kampf.* According to his book, Germany and the great Nordic or Aryan race lost World War I because of the treason of liberals, Jews, and Bolsheviks. The great German Empire had been replaced by the pathetic Weimar Republic, led by the very people who he claimed had betrayed Germany.

When Hitler was released from prison after only nine months of confinement, the German economic situation had improved. The Nazis might have disappeared had it not been for the Great Depression. When millions became unemployed in 1930 and bread lines formed, Hitler was delighted. His party promised jobs, food, and national pride. In 1928 only 12 Reichstag deputies were Nazis, but in 1930, 107 Nazis were elected, and in 1932 they won 230 seats, making Hitler's the largest single party in Germany. In January 1933 President Hindenburg named Hitler as chancellor.

Hitler's lieutenants constantly battled among themselves. Ernst Röhm led the SA Brown Shirts, a military group that supported Hitler. They had been useful when Hitler was outside government, but now Hitler was the führer (leader) and needed the support of wealthy industrialists and the aristocrats. A new elite group was picked from the best of the SAs in 1930: the SS, headed by Heinrich Himmler. They were better educated, from more respectable families, and very loyal to Hitler. To take charge of information gathering, Himmler created the SD under Reinhard Heydrich. Spies and informers gave Heydrich the information that he needed to justify Röhm's arrest. On June 30, 1934, the "Night of the Long Knives," Röhm and 200 other SA men were arrested and executed.

In 1936 Hitler named Himmler head of all police in Germany. There were not only ordinary police, but also criminal police and political police (gestapo). Political prisoners were sent to a new concentration camp at Dachau, which was a few miles from Munich. Since Dachau held only 5,000 prisoners and many new customers were being picked up every week, other camps were built, the most famous being Buchenwald.

SS units created fear in Germany and silenced all but the bravest. Ministers and priests were watched carefully. If they criticized Hitler's policies, they were sent to concentration camps. Many of them died there. The SS followed the army during invasions, going after Jews, gypsies, union leaders, Communists, or those listed as "subhumans."

Selling the Nazi regime to foreigners and the nation was the job of Foreign Minister Joachim von Ribbentrop and Dr. Joseph Goebbels, minister of propaganda. Neither worried about lies or deception. The world was faced with a government based on hate and fear with no conscience to trouble it. Nazi Germany joined Japan and Italy in creating wars.

Debate in 1936

The situation in Germany is serious, and the United States should take a major part in ending the Nazi regime.

10

Name_____ Date _____

POINTS TO CONSIDER

1. Would the Weimar Republic have been better off if it had kept prisoners like Hitler in jail for their full term or simply executed them?

_____

_____

_____

_____

_____

2. Why do you think the Depression created so much violence in Germany?

_____

_____

_____

_____

_____

3. What did the "Night of the Long Knives" say about the Nazi Party?

_____

_____

_____

_____

_____

Name_____ Date _____

CHALLENGES

1. Were the Spartacists a branch of the Nazi Party?

_____

2. What were the two houses of the German parliament? Underline the one that was elected by popular vote.

_____

3. What was the official name for the Nazi Party?

_____

4. What religious group and what party did Nazis especially hate?

_____

_____

5. By what other name were the SA known?

_____

6. According to *Mein Kampf*, what groups had caused Germany's defeat in World War I?

_____

_____

7. How many more seats did the Nazis have in the Reichstag in 1932 than they had in 1928?

_____

8. Why were the SA a problem for Chancellor Hitler?

_____

_____

9. How was that problem solved?

_____

_____

10. What were two concentration camps established by the gestapo?

_____

_____

THE WINDS OF WAR BEGIN TO BLOW

The inflated egos of dictators lead them to raise large armies. These defend the nation and intimidate any rivals. To justify large armies and navies, each dictator needs an enemy who is "threatening" the security of the nation. If that enemy is eliminated, then others must be found. Powerful nations are watching, so the dictator must find a pretext for attacking this weaker "enemy" nation. From 1931 to 1939 the dictators were on the prowl, picking off weak neighbors and justifying their actions with innocent faces.

A Japanese soldier

On Septmeber 18, 1931, Japanese agents staged an explosion under the tracks of the Japanese-owned South Manchurian Railway. So little damage was done that a train crossed over the track a few minutes later. Nonetheless, Japan blamed the incident on the Chinese, and their troops seized Manchuria. Japan's intention of keeping Manchuria was made clear when they renamed it Manchukuo and set up a puppet government under Japanese control there. The League of Nations passed timid resolutions against Japan, so Japan left the League. U.S. protests did little except stir up anti-U.S. feeling in Japan.

After Germany's Night of the Long Knives, SS agents killed Austria's Chancellor Dollfuss in July 1934. Mussolini sent troops to the Austrian border to protect it from *Anschluss* by Germany. Other nations praised Mussolini's actions. Mussolini felt his support of Austria justified his seizure of Ethiopia on Africa's east coast. In 1887 and 1896 the Italians had been humiliated in defeats by Ethiopia and looked for excuses to redeem their honor. After small border incidents provoked by the Italians, Mussolini threatened war with Ethiopia. The League voted to impose economic sanctions (trade restrictions) if Italy attacked. Mussolini used the sanctions to arouse Italian patriotic fervor to new heights.

In October 1935 Italian forces attacked Ethiopia. The Ethiopians fought bravely, but their spears and arrows bounced off Italian tanks. The League imposed sanctions against Italy but left petroleum off the list. Little effort was made to enforce the sanctions anyway. In May 1936 the Ethiopian capital, Addis Ababa, fell, and Mussolini bragged: "Ethiopia is Italian—Italian in fact, because occupied by our victorious armies, and Italian by right because, with the sword of Rome, civilization has triumphed over barbarism." Rodolfo Graziani was named governor. He killed most of the Coptic church leaders and the best-educated Ethiopians.

While the world watched the conquest of Ethiopia, the French were in one of their emergency cabinet crises. In March 1936 Hitler sent 35,000 troops into the demilitarized Rhineland. He was clearly violating the Treaty of Versailles, the Locarno Pacts, and all other restrictions to which Germany had agreed. It was pure bluff. "If the French had marched into the Rhineland," Hitler wrote, "we would have had to withdraw with our tails between our legs." France did nothing and Hitler gloated.

The Spanish Civil War began in 1936, and both sides received outside support. The Spanish Republicans were aided by France and Russia, and Franco's Fascists were aided by Italy and Germany. Hitler sent the 100-plane Condor Legion. Mussolini sent some aircraft but helped more with soldiers. Both sent tanks and artillery. From 1936 to 1938 Stalin sold the Republicans tanks and aircraft. The Communist International Party recruited volunteers for the Republican cause. Many of these were Communists, but others were not. The war ended in 1939 with a Fascist triumph.

The common effort in Spain brought Hitler and Mussolini together. In September 1937 Hitler invited Il Duce to Germany for a meeting that developed a strong friendship between the two Fascist leaders. Mussolini returned from the visit with new ideas about toughening up the Italians. In 1936 Germany and Japan had signed an Anti-Comintern Axis (alliance). In November 1937 Italy became the third Axis nation.

Austria, lying between Germany and Italy, had only Italy to help it stay independent. With Italy now friendly, Hitler was free to pressure Austria into becoming part of Germany. Chancellor Kurt Schuschnigg tried to maintain Austrian independence, but caved in on March 11, 1938. Hitler declared Anschluss, and Austria became part of the German Reich.

Now Czechoslovakia was in the jaws of the tiger. The 3.5 million German-speaking Sudetens were unhappy under Czech rule and wanted German rule. Since the Czechs had alliances with France and Russia, much depended on their reactions. To protect Germany from French attack, Hitler began building defenses on the border (the West Wall or Siegfried Line). In September 1938 Hitler said that the Sudetens had a right to choose German rule, but he could not long be indifferent to their suffering. English Prime Minister Chamberlain and Premier Daladier of France met with Hitler and Mussolini at Munich in September 1938. To prevent a war they were incapable of fighting at the time, England and France gave in and told Czechoslovakia to accept German terms. Chamberlain returned to England as a hero and, waving the agreement in his hand, told the world that he had achieved "peace in our time." Without Western support the Czechs had no choice except to give in.

Possessing the most valuable industrial region of Czechoslovakia, it was easy for Hitler to take the rest of the nation in March 1939. Poland now faced the might of Nazi Germany. England and France warned Germany that an attack on Poland would mean war.

Debate

Was World War II inevitable after the Munich Conference?

Name _____ Date _____

POINTS TO CONSIDER

1. Why do nations that invade their neighbors try to find an excuse for what they are doing?

_____

_____

_____

_____

_____

2. Why would sending troops, tanks, and planes be of use to the nations getting involved in the Spanish Civil War?

_____

_____

_____

_____

_____

3. At what points could Hitler have been stopped from 1933 to 1938? Why wasn't he?

_____

_____

_____

_____

_____

Name_____ Date _____

CHALLENGES

1. What was Japan's excuse for seizing Manchuria from the Chinese?

_____

_____

2. What name did the Japanese give Manchuria?

_____

3. Who prevented an Anschluss in 1934?

_____

4. What weapons did the Ethiopians have against the Italians?

_____

5. What agreements did Hitler violate by his invasion of the Rhineland?

_____

6. What would have happened if the French had opposed the invasion?

_____

_____

7. What four foreign nations got involved in the Spanish Civil War? Underline those helping the Republicans.

_____

8. What agreement brought Germany, Japan, and Italy together?

_____

9. What nations were part of the Anschluss?

_____

10. What was Hitler's excuse for seizing the Sudeten?

_____

_____

_____

THE OPENING SALVOS OF WWII

China had known no peace since 1911. First the Nationalists (KMT) led by Chiang Kai-shek battled warlords; then the KMT fought Mao Zedong's Communists (CCP). Japan took advantage of the turmoil by invading Manchuria in 1931, landing troops near Shanghai in 1932, and continuing to drive farther into northern China. China's leaders devoted less attention to the Japanese than to continuing their own fight. The KMT held the upper hand and in 1934 forced Mao's followers to begin their Long March to safety. Chiang was generally accepted as China's legitimate leader, and he began building a stronger transportation network and larger industrial capacity.

Japan much preferred a weak China and used an incident at the Marco Polo Bridge near Beijing as the excuse to invade China in 1937.

In June 1940 France surrendered to the Germans.

That was followed by massacres of civilians at Shanghai and Nanjing. China's only hope was for its armies to stop fighting each other, so a truce was arranged. Still, both the CCP and KMT devoted more effort to outflanking each other than fighting the Japanese. For Japan, China was a problem since so many troops were tied down holding the territory they had seized.

In 1939 Hitler carefully planned his move against Poland. England and France had warned that an attack would mean war. Russia was geographically able to help Poland if it chose. To the amazement of the world, the Nazi Germans signed a nonaggression deal with the Communist Russians. They agreed to divide Poland between them, and the Russians were allowed to take the three Baltic republics (Estonia, Latvia, and Lithuania) as well.

Hitler now left no doubt of his intentions. In August 1939 he told his officers: "Close heart to pity. Proceed brutally." Before Hitler attacked Poland, however, he needed an excuse. In Operation Canned Goods, inmates of a concentration camp dressed in Polish army uniforms "attacked" a German radio station at Gleiwitz. The Germans attacked Poland the next day, September 1. All raid participants were killed to prevent information leaks.

Hitler hoped England and France would not interfere, but the British and French declared war on September 3. For the Poles, this brought little comfort. Hitler's *blitzkrieg* (lightning war) tactic was highly effective. Blitzkrieg began with massive air attacks destroying air cover, hitting communication centers, and terrorizing cities. Armored units then hit before defenders could get on their feet again. The Poles fought with no outside help. The odds were overwhelming. Within three weeks, the Nazis had gone past the line they had drawn with Stalin, then moved back to the agreed-upon line. Russian troops moved into eastern Poland. About 200,000 Poles escaped. Many made it to England where they fought beside

17

the Allies.

Even though England and France were supposedly at war with Germany, at first there was no fighting. Hitler said: "I have neither toward England nor France any war claims, nor has the German nation." But not even Prime Minister Chamberlain bought that. He said that England's purpose was "to redeem Europe from the . . . fear of German aggression."

While Hitler talked peace, he planned his next moves. The French stayed secure behind their Maginot (defense) Line, which guarded the French-German boundary. The 250 miles between Belgium and France were unprotected, however. Across from France's 70 divisions and 3,000 tanks were 33 German divisions without tanks. All France needed was the will to fight, but it had none. England's Royal Air Force (RAF) sat on the ground because the German targets it could reach were private property. This response was scoffed at as *sitzkrieg,* because the English were simply sitting and doing nothing.

The German invasion of Denmark and Norway on April 9, 1940, ended talk of sitzkrieg. Denmark was overrun before anyone knew it. Norway was harder for the Germans to defeat, even though they had an active underground there led by Vidkum Quisling. The Norwegians, with the help of English and French paratroopers, stubbornly fought General Dietl's German troops. British failure in Norway doomed Prime Minister Chamberlain, and Winston Churchill replaced him May 10. On June 10 Norway surrendered.

On May 9, 1940, blitzkrieg struck again as the Germans attacked the Dutch and Belgians. The Dutch were easily overwhelmed; they had depended on flooded dikes to hold the Germans off, but transport planes cancelled that defense. The queen escaped on May 13 and all resistance ended. Belgium received some support from the English and French, but their collapse was so quick that the troops sent to help were trapped and withdrew to Dunkirk. Belgium was lost in eight days. A heroic effort by the Royal Navy and volunteers using boats of all sorts rescued the 337,000 Allied soldiers at Dunkirk from May 26 to June 4.

The Weygand Line was supposed to protect the rest of France. In some places, it prevented an easy German invasion, but behind the front line there were no reserves to plug a break in the line. On June 21 the Germans presented surrender terms to the French; the surrender took place in the same railroad car where Germans had signed the armistice in 1918. France was to be divided; Germany occupied northern France, and southern France would be governed from Vichy by a puppet government. General Charles DeGaulle escaped to England and established the Free French army.

Debate

Were the French and English doing the right thing when they offered no help to Poland in 1939?

Name_____ Date _____

POINTS TO CONSIDER

1. "Total war" involves attacks on civilians as well as armies. How does it affect the way wars are fought?

_____

_____

_____

_____

_____

2. As a person in France in 1940, would you have favored attacking the Germans while they were still relatively weak on the western front?

_____

_____

_____

_____

_____

3. Why did Hitler take special delight in forcing the French to surrender in that particular railroad car?

_____

_____

_____

_____

_____

Name_____ Date _____

CHALLENGES

1. What leader was the KMT battling while the Japanese marched into China?

_____

2. What Chinese cities suffered bloody civilian massacres in 1937?

_____

3. Why did Hitler need to worry about England and France before he attacked Poland?

_____

_____

4. Why did Hitler execute those who participated in the raid on Gleiwitz?

_____

_____

5. What were the first and second waves of a blitzkrieg attack?

_____

6. What defense line had France built along the German border?

_____

7. Would the French have had the odds in their favor if they had attacked in 1939?

_____

8. The lack of fighting along the western front was called the "phony war" by some. By what other name was it also known?

_____

9. What helped the German attack on Norway?

_____

_____

10. What made Dunkirk important in the war?

_____

_____

THE WAR SPREADS

The United States was like an island surrounded by angry seas during the first two years of the war. It was neither isolated from danger nor neutral in its sympathies, however. Short of direct involvement, most Americans were willing to help the peaceful nations under attack.

The evacuation (leaving) of Dunkirk in 1940 was a good example. The troops were rescued, but 7,000 tons of ammunition, 90,000 rifles, and 120,000 vehicles were left behind. President Roosevelt asked the army and navy to send a list of whatever weapons

St. Paul's Cathedral in London survived the Battle of Britain.

could be spared. After the list was approved by General George Marshall, the goods were sold to the British for $37 million. Even with American help, it was feared the British might still be overpowered by a German invasion.

In November 1940 the Russians attacked Finland with 45 divisions along the whole border. The Finnish army was small (about 175,000–200,000 men) but was prepared for the cold (about -50°F) and held off about one million Russians. England, France, and the United States thought about helping the Finns, but no aid was sent. Congress offered to lend $30 million for Finland to buy civilian supplies and farm equipment, but that was not what the Finns needed. The Finns were finally overcome and gave in to Soviet demands for a border line with more space between Finland and Leningrad.

Minister of War Hideko Tojo of Japan was also looking for more space for his nation and an end to Western influence in Asia. Part of his plan involved taking bases in northern French Indo-China (Vietnam) from the puppet Vichy government in 1940. The United States angrily responded by sending another $25 million in supplies to help China.

With the *Luftwaffe* (German air force) flying high, the Nazis said it would put a "steel roof over Germany." It, along with the *Wehrmacht* (army) and its *Panzer* (armored) divisions, were battle tested by 1940. Hitler had hoped to win England as an ally, but his brutal treatment of Europe had silenced most of his former British supporters.

For Operation Sea Lion (the invasion of England) to succeed, Hitler had to master the air, and that would only be possible by destroying the Royal Air Force (RAF). Göring gave his fliers several tasks: destroy shipping and the RAF and terrorize cities. The Germans had about 2,600 planes (including 1,480 bombers and 980 fighters) to use in this attack. "Eagle Day," the beginning of the Battle of Britain, came August 13, 1940. "Britain's finest hour," as Churchill called it, depended on brave men and high-quality fighter planes.

The British used Hurricanes and Spitfires; their attackers had Heinkel bombers, Stuka (JU-87) dive bombers, and ME–109 and ME–110 fighters. Radar spotted the enemy planes coming and relayed the report to the squadron. The "scramble" signal was given; the squadron was off the ground in 2 or 3 minutes and 15 minutes later was flying at 20,000 feet.

Churchill wrote that German planes were faster and climbed better, but that English planes were more manueverable and better armed.

In late August, Hitler gave up on persuading Churchill to come to the bargaining table. London itself would be the new target. Attacks on London began September 7. For the first two days, the Luftwaffe controlled the skies and Göring gloated: "London is on fire." The damage reports were exaggerated, but the Luftwaffe had met little opposition and civilians had been killed. Hitler hoped this would weaken the English will to fight, but the attacks only served to strengthen English determination.

The most spectacular night of the "blitz" was September 15, when 200 bombers supported by fighter planes crossed the English Channel. The RAF had brought up all its reserves, and a deadly game took place in the skies. When it was over, the Germans had lost about 60 planes to the RAF's 26. The next day, the German high command decided that England was far from defeated and Channel seas would be too rough for landing craft to invade until spring. Hitler called off the invasion until further notice. Air attacks continued on English cities, the most spectacular being that of Coventry. Americans kept up with the news through radio newscasts and newsreels and wondered if the United States could stay out of the war.

Every presidential contest in the United States has its unique qualities, and the 1940 election was no exception. Roosevelt (often called FDR) was running for a third term, something no president had ever tried. His Republican opponent, Wendell Willkie, had been a Democrat until 1938. Willkie hated fascism and did not want to say anything that would hurt aid to England or encourage Hitler. In September when FDR sent 50 old destroyers to England in return for leases of naval bases in the Western Hemisphere, Willkie supported the aid.

Willkie's campaign moved slowly until he attacked FDR's promises to "keep our boys out of the war." Willkie said if these promises were no better kept than those to balance the budget, the boys were already "almost on the transports." In October he predicted that Roosevelt would have the nation in the war by April 1940. FDR said: "I have said this before, but I shall say it again . . . Your boys are not going to be sent to any foreign wars." When asked about leaving off the condition "except in case of attack," he said: "If somebody attacks us, then it isn't a foreign war."

Debate in 1940

FDR's policies are doomed to get us into the war.

Name_____ Date _____

POINTS TO CONSIDER

1. A neutral nation is one that does not take sides during a war. Was the United States truly neutral in 1940?

_____

_____

_____

_____

_____

2. What difference do slogans make during a war?

_____

_____

_____

_____

_____

3. Why was Willkie's accusation that Roosevelt would not keep his promise to keep Americans out of the war not helpful to his campaign?

_____

_____

_____

_____

_____

Name_____ Date _____

CHALLENGES

1. Why were the English short of supplies in 1940?

_____

_____

2. How many Russians did it take to defeat the Finns in 1940?

_____

3. What area was Tojo interested in taking in 1940?

_____

4. What were the names of the German air force, army, and armored divisions?

_____

_____

5. What three jobs did Göring assign to the Luftwaffe?

_____

6. Why was August 13 significant to the British?

_____

_____

7. What were the two fighter planes England relied on, and which fighters did the Luftwaffe use most (underline the German planes)?

_____

_____

8. How many more planes did the Luftwaffe lose on September 15 than the RAF did?

_____

9. What was the importance of that air raid?

_____

_____

10. What did the United States get in return for the 50 destroyers?

_____

TWO GIANTS ENTER THE WAR

With war raging in Europe and the Far East, the USSR and United States were too close to danger to feel safe. The Russians remembered that 1.7 million of their men had died while fighting in World War I. The casualties of the recent war with the Finns reminded any who had forgotten.

The United States wanted to stay neutral. In the 1930s Congress tried to avoid the mis-

Eight battleships were either sunk or badly damaged by the Japanese at Pearl Harbor.

takes that had drawn the nation into World War I. Between 1935 and 1937, Congress passed a series of Neutrality Acts. These ordered the president to embargo (stop selling) arms to belligerents (nations at war), forbade belligerents to borrow money in the United States, and prohibited U.S. merchant ships from carrying munitions to belligerents. The president also required all purchases to be "cash and carry" and forbade enemy warships and armed merchant ships to enter U.S. ports.

The United States realized that the Axis must have no bases in the Western Hemisphere. At the Havana Conference in 1940, the 21 nations of the Pan-American Conference agreed that no European nation could transfer its Western Hemisphere colonies to another non-American nation. That kept French, Dutch, and Danish colonies out of German hands. Also that year, the United States and Canada (which was already in the war) formed a defense board to study sea, land, and air defenses of the northern Western Hemisphere.

After the U.S. presidential election, Roosevelt followed a policy that was barely neutral. The Lend-Lease program was based on the idea of helping a friend through a difficult time. If his house is on fire, you lend a hose. When the crisis is over, your hose is returned. The Lend-Lease Act passed by Congress in March 1941 allowed Britain to borrow up to $7 billion worth of American equipment. That, along with the Selective Service Act (the first peacetime draft in U.S. history) and increased defense spending made it clear the United States was not sure it could stay out of the war.

In the Kremlin, Stalin rested secure in his nonaggression agreement with Hitler. But after finding England too tough to conquer, Hitler decided to pick on Russia instead. Students of history knew what had happened to Napoleon when he tried the same thing in 1812, but Hitler was confident that modern war machines could cancel supply problems and Russian weather. He believed that after Russia was defeated, England would give up or be invaded.

Hitler could justify the attack on military grounds. Half of Germany's petroleum came from the Ploesti refineries in Romania, well within range of Russian bombers. A defeated Russia could be forced to supply him with the grain, minerals, and petroleum his *Wehrmacht* needed. Rubber and tin could be shipped from the Far East through a humbled Russia to supply German needs. Besides, it would create a comfortable *Lebensraum* (living room or

25

space) to protect Germany from a surprise attack from the east. German generals began preparing for the invasion, code named Operation Barbarossa.

The United States and England warned Stalin that the attack was coming, but he did not listen. On June 22, 1941, 1,800 planes, 600,000 vehicles, and 3,000 tanks struck. The Russian line yielded quickly, and Germans advanced at alarming speeds. U.S. Lend-Lease aid now flowed into Russia as well.

Sending supplies through the North Atlantic was hazardous because of German "wolf packs" of U-boats (submarines). These were sinking merchant ships faster than U.S. and British shipyards built them. U.S. naval ships escorted transports for longer distances, with the Royal Navy escorting them the last leg of the journey. These missions became increasingly hazardous. On September 24, 1941, the destroyer *U.S.S. Greer* was helping the Royal Navy search for U-boats when a sub fired a torpedo at it. The order that U.S. ships were not to fire on U-boats was lifted. Now they could shoot on sight. But in October the *U.S.S. Kearny* and the *U.S.S. Reuben James* were sunk off Iceland, and a total of 126 crewmen died.

Since the gunboat *U.S.S. Panay* had been sunk by Japanese aircraft in 1937, it had been clear that the United States and Japan were not friendly. Relations had worsened after Japan invaded all of Indo-China in July 1941; the United States then froze all Japanese assets. Diplomatic exchanges continued but went nowhere. The order was given by General Tojo of Japan on November 26, 1941, for six aircraft carriers and 25 support ships to attack Pearl Harbor on December 7.

December 7 was a day of blunders for both sides. The American commanders at Pearl Harbor made many mistakes: ignoring radar reports, holding up the report that a small sub had been sunk at the harbor entrance, lining up planes in a straight line down runways at Hickam Field, and sending a message to be on the alert through Western Union without an "urgent" label attached. The United States paid for it on the morning of December 7 when the attackers sank or damaged eight battleships, ten other navy ships, and 187 planes. The U.S. carriers were at sea, so they were not harmed in the attack.

For the Japanese, Pearl Harbor was an even greater day of blunders. They failed to take seriously the warnings of General Yamashita and Admiral Yamamoto against tangling with the United States. The warning that an attack was coming was not delivered to Yamamoto until 55 minutes after the attack began. When he learned of the attack, he said: "I can't imagine anything that would infuriate the Americans more. I fear all we have done is to awaken a sleeping giant, and fill him with a terrible resolve."

Debate

Roosevelt had done everything possible to keep the United States out of the war.

Name_____ Date _____

POINTS TO CONSIDER

1. Keeping in mind the Italian attack on Ethiopia, the Japanese attack on China, and the German invasion of Czechoslovakia, were the neutrality laws that were passed useful?

_____

_____

_____

_____

_____

2. One congressman said that Lend-Lease was like lending chewing gum—you wouldn't want it back after it was used. What point was he making?

_____

_____

_____

_____

_____

3. Did Hitler have grounds for attacking American destroyers in 1941?

_____

_____

_____

_____

_____

Name_____ Date _____

CHALLENGES

1. The Nye Committee of the Senate accused the bankers of being responsible for the United States entering World War I. What part of the Neutrality Acts prevented that from happening again?

_____

2. The English liner *Lusitania* was sunk in 1915 while carrying munitions as well as passengers to England. How would the Neutrality Acts prevent U.S. ships from getting involved in that situation?

_____

3. What European nations conquered by the Germans had colonies in the Western Hemisphere?

_____

4. With what nation did the United States develop plans to defend the northern part of the Western Hemisphere?

_____

5. What situation was Lend-Lease similar to?

_____

_____

6. Who else had tried to invade Russia?

_____

7. What was the purpose of Operation Barbarossa?

_____

_____

8. Name three U.S. ships attacked by U-boats.

_____

9. How many Japanese ships were involved in the attack on Pearl Harbor?

_____

10. What Japanese leaders had warned that the attack would be a mistake?

_____

GOLIATHS FALL TO SLINGSHOTS: THE NAVAL WAR

The battleship *Bismarck* was the pride of the German fleet.

In the tight budget days between the two world wars, some looked on navies as useless. The easy way to cut military expenses was to stop building big ships. In 1928 the most outspoken critic of navies was General Billy Mitchell. He said that air power was already ahead of land or sea power. The best sea weapon, he contended, was the submarine, and the best defense against a submarine was another submarine. Although in World War II surface craft were necessary, Mitchell claimed that submarines would menace surface fleets and merchant ships carrying war supplies across the ocean.

Old navy men were not convinced at all by the critics. Navies had helped win many wars, and the more powerful the ship, the more it could accomplish. The pride of the world's fleets were their battleships. Yet, one by one, these majestic monuments were removed from the active list.

The Royal Navy entered the war with 15 battleships, but the *H.M.S. Royal Oak* was sunk while sitting in its harbor in October 1939 by a German U-boat (submarine). The German's *Graf Spee* slipped through the British blockade in 1939. Heading for the South Atlantic, she led her pursuers on a long chase ending at the Rio de la Plata in South America. Damaged after battling three British cruisers, she entered the Montevideo harbor for repairs. The Uruguayan government allowed only 72 hours for her to leave. The captain was commanded to either fight his way out or scuttle the ship. He scuttled the ship on December 17.

The pride of the German fleet was the *Bismarck.* Accompanied by the smaller *Prinz Eugene,* she sailed out to attack British shipping in the North Atlantic in April 1941. Smaller British ships buzzed around her until the battleships *George V* and *Rodney* could be brought into the fight. On May 26 the *Bismarck* rolled over, killing most of its crew.

The U.S. Navy had 15 battleships until Pearl Harbor, when three were destroyed and five badly damaged. This did more harm to pride than to the ability to fight. Admiral Yamamoto and other intelligent Japanese naval men knew the Pearl Harbor raid had failed when they learned that no aircraft carriers were in port that day. While part of the Japanese fleet was involved in the attack on Pearl Harbor, other ships were moving toward the Philippines, Thailand, and Malaysia. As Japanese troops advanced toward Singapore, the *H.M.S. Prince of Wales* and the cruiser *Repulse* tried to stop them. The carrier *Indominatable* was to have escorted them, but it was damaged, so the ships had no air cover. They were sunk by Japanese dive and torpedo bombers on December 10, 1941.

Allied losses in the Pacific caused U.S. chief of naval operations, Admiral Ernest King, to say: "The plain facts of the matter are that we have not the 'tools' wherewith to meet the enemy at all points he is threatening;—Hawaii *must* be held—we must do what we can to maintain the line of communications with Australia."

In the Atlantic the losses hurting the Allies were not battleships, but merchant ships. The U-boats, commanded by Admiral Donitz, played havoc with supplies along the U.S. Atlantic coast, between the United States and England, and between England and the Russian port at Murmansk. Using only a handful of U-boats at a time, the Germans sank 492 ships off the U.S. eastern seaboard between January 12 and June 30, 1942. Since coastal merchantships and tankers operated alone and without escort, they made easy targets, especially when cities did not turn off lights around harbors because it might hurt the tourist trade. By July 1942 the army air force had 141 planes available to hunt subs, and the navy had 178 planes and seven blimps. These operated out of 26 bases from Newfoundland to Jacksonville, Florida. In the Gulf of Mexico area, the army had 62 planes and the navy had 96.

Ships crossing the Atlantic were in danger of U-boat "wolf packs," which would surface and attack the ships at night. Deck guns were often used by U-boat crews to conserve their supply of torpedoes. The most dangerous run of all was between England and Russia because ships could be attacked by land-based *Luftwaffe* as well as submarines. Admiral Samuel Eliot Morison reported that of 301 ships sailing from August 1941 through December 1942, 53 were lost. About half of those lost were American.

Several solutions were found to combat the wolf packs. Radar was used by the Allies on land, sea, and air. As it improved in quality, it made the submariner's profession more hazardous. Code breakers were also very helpful. The German Enigma code was broken by the Poles, and Operation Magic broke the Japanese Purple Code. In addition, the Coastal Picket Patrol (CPP or "Hooligan Navy") was made up of privately owned yachts, boats, and small freighters who would watch for and report any conning towers or periscopes they saw. The Civil Air Patrol (CAP) performed much the same function from the air. Both the CPP and CAP were made up of civilians who were not eligible for the draft because of age or disabilities. Thus, both highly sophisticated and amateur means challenged the submarine threat.

Admiral Morison's conclusion about the naval war in the Atlantic was that the U.S. Navy "was woefully unprepared, materially and mentally, for the U-boat blitz on the Atlantic Coast that began in January 1942." The navy corrected its errors in a few months but not until many merchant ships had been sunk because of early mistakes.

Debate

Civilian volunteers should not be endangered by involvement in national defense.

Name _____ Date _____

POINTS TO CONSIDER

1. Why were battleships losing their appeal from 1939 to 1941?

_____

_____

_____

_____

_____

2. If you were Admiral King in 1942, what "tools" would you ask for?

_____

_____

_____

_____

_____

3. A convoy of 25 ships is going across the ocean, and you are in charge of escorting them with six destroyers. Where will you place the escort ships at night?

_____

_____

_____

_____

_____

Name_____ Date _____

CHALLENGES

1. What did General Mitchell believe was the most useful naval weapon, and what did he believe was the best defense against it?

_____

_____

2. In what nation did Germany's *Graf Spee* meet its end?

_____

3. What battleships were used to sink the *Bismarck?*

_____

4. How many U.S. battleships were ready to fight the day after Pearl Harbor?

_____

5. Why didn't the *Prince of Wales* have air cover?

_____

_____

6. What two goals did Admiral King set?

_____

_____

7. The time span from January 12 to June 30 is 169 days. How many ships were sunk each day off the U.S. seaboard during that period in 1942?

_____

8. Why did U-boats use deck guns rather than torpedoes in attacking convoys?

_____

_____

9. Name two enemy codes that were broken early in the war. Underline the German code.

_____

10. What was the official name for the "Hooligan Navy"?

_____

LOSING AND WINNING SOME IN THE PACIFIC

The aircraft carrier U.S.S. Lexington had to be abandoned during the Battle of the Coral Sea

In 1941 and 1942 Japan seemed to be like a balloon expanding in every direction at the same time. The islands of the Dutch East Indies (now Indonesia), with their vast oil deposits, were obvious targets for Japan, a nation with no oil. The British colonies were almost undefended since most troops had been recalled to save England; Malaysia and Burma had little protection. India was restless with nationalism, and Australia and New Zealand were bracing for the storm they knew was coming from the north.

The United States sent what help it could to its allies in the Far East. At first supplies to China were sent northward from Rangoon to Lashio, Burma, and then over the "Burma Road," 700 miles of hairpin-curved mountain roads to Kunming, China. In 1942 Rangoon fell, and Japanese troops captured Lashio. The only route for goods then was "over the hump"–the Himalayas. Flying over the Himalayas in a little C–47 with a ceiling of 24,100 feet was so risky that it was known as the "Aluminum Trail."

At the time of the attack on Pearl Harbor, U.S. forces in the Philippines numbered about 135,000. Commanded by General Douglas MacArthur, most were stationed on the main island of Luzon. Major defenses protecting Manila were on the Bataan Peninsula west of the harbor and the small island of Corregidor in the bay leading to the city. The Japanese attacked the major U.S. airport, Clark Field, on December 8, destroying most of its B–17s on the ground. Two days later the Japanese bombed Manila. General Homma's Fourteenth Army moved into northern Luzon and easily shoved the half-trained Filipino troops aside. MacArthur withdrew to the Bataan defense line and demanded more troops and air support from General Marshall.

The support he wanted was not coming. Roosevelt and Churchill had agreed in the Arcadia Conference that Hitler must be defeated first, and U.S. resources were going to beef up the defense of England. FDR sent a message to President Quezon of the Philippines that spoke of his determination to free the islands as soon as possible: "We shall not relax our efforts until the forces which are now marshalling outside the Philippines . . . drive out the last remnant of invaders from your soil." Bataan was doomed. MacArthur was ordered in February to go to Australia, where he took command of all U.S. troops in the Pacific. There he promised: "I shall return."

With success everywhere, the Japanese were getting too cocky to suit U.S. lieutenant colonel Jimmy Doolittle. He designed a B–25 bomber raid on Tokyo, with his planes taking off from the aircraft carrier *Hornet.* The *Hornet* was spotted at sea, and the Japanese public was warned but paid little attention. The 16 planes did little damage, but their attack showed that the mainland was in danger, so four fighter groups were assigned to protect Japan from the attacks that no one in the United States had planned.

Back in the Philippines, General Jonathan Wainwright was left in command. Bataan fell in April, and Corregidor was surrendered in May 1942. The 70,000 starved prisoners captured on Bataan were forced to walk 60 miles in sweltering heat to the nearest railroad; 17,000 were killed or died of hunger or thirst on the infamous "Bataan Death March."

North of Australia and east of New Guinea lie the Coral Sea and the Solomon Islands. The Japanese capture of Rabaul at the eastern tip of New Britain Island in January 1942 threatened the supply line to Australia. The Japanese prepared Operation Mo to take Port Moresby. From this port, Australia could be attacked. Since the Japanese naval code had been broken, however, Admiral Chester Nimitz knew their plans and prepared a defense.

The Japanese and U.S. fleets each had two aircraft carriers (the U.S. carriers were the *Lexington* and *Yorktown*), and the United States outnumbered the Japanese in the air 122 to 121. Both fleets suffered major losses in the Battle of the Coral Sea. The *Lexington* was so badly damaged by torpedoes fired from Japanese planes that it was scuttled. The Japanese carrier *Shokaku* was damaged and had to withdraw. The Battle of the Coral Sea was important for two reasons: it was the first naval battle ever fought completely by airplanes, and this was the first time a Japanese invasion had been blocked. Neither Japanese aircraft carrier could be used at the upcoming battle at Midway Island.

Midway Island lay about 1,000 miles northwest of the Hawaiian Islands. Admiral Yamamoto planned to bring a powerful Japanese fleet there, attack by surprise, and pull the U.S. fleet out to battle. With a larger force, Japan would rule the Pacific for many years to come. Admiral Nimitz knew what he was planning thanks to the Operation Magic code breaker. The Japanese fleet included 8 carriers, 11 battleships, 18 cruisers, and 65 destroyers; the U.S. fleet had 3 carriers, 8 cruisers, and 15 destroyers. As at the Coral Sea, ships never fired on each other and planes did all the damage. While the *Yorktown* was being pounded by planes from the *Hiruyu,* the *Hiruyu* was under attack by planes from the *Enterprise.* The *Yorktown* was the only American carrier lost in the battle. Japan lost four carriers and suffered its first naval defeat since 1594. Japan was losing its advantage in the Pacific.

Debate

U.S. troops should have been pulled out of the Philippines before the situation there became hopeless.

Name_____ Date _____

POINTS TO CONSIDER

1. As MacArthur, how would you have felt about the Arcadia Conference?

_____

_____

_____

_____

2. Why were the battles of the Coral Sea and Midway important from both a military and a psychological point of view?

_____

_____

_____

_____

3. How did the war in the Pacific show the value of code breakers?

_____

_____

_____

_____

Name _____ Date _____

CHALLENGES

1. Name two countries that were in danger of Japanese attack.

_____

2. What was the first supply route to China called?

_____

3. What was the nickname for the Himalayas?

_____

4. What were the two major defensive positions for the U.S. Army in the Philippines?

_____

_____

5. Who said: "I shall return"?

_____

6. Who planned and carried out the B-25 raid on Tokyo?

_____

7. How many captured Americans died on the Bataan Death March?

_____

8. What U.S. aircraft carrier was badly damaged in the Battle of the Coral Sea?

_____

9. What made the Battle of the Coral Sea unusual in naval history?

_____

_____

10. What Japanese carrier was under attack at Midway while its planes were away?

_____

THE GERMAN ADVANCE TO THE GATES OF MOSCOW

Russian defenders sent out Vickers eight-ton tanks to battle the Germans.

It seems odd that Stalin, who trusted no one, was surprised by Hitler's betrayal of the nonaggression pact, but after reports came in that German troops were attacking (Operation Barbarossa), he did nothing for five days. During that time the *Luftwaffe* destroyed 4,000 Russian planes, many of them on the ground. The *Wehrmacht* marched into the Baltic states, eastern Poland, and the Ukraine. This began one of the bloodiest campaigns of the war. Hitler told his troops that the struggle was to be conducted with "unmerciful and unrelenting harshness." The treatment of Russian prisoners was seconded only by that of Japanese prisoner of war (POW) camps.

As in past wars, Russian defeats were not the fault of the soldiers as fighting men. The fault lay squarely in the nation's leadership. Stalin himself was responsible for some of this. He had put political concerns over military in his army. Political commissars watched military officers to make sure they did not stray from party teachings. Generals' roles declined during the war, but none made a decision without a tattletale by his side. Failure or retreat was treated as treason.

The purges of the 1930s had caused some of the best military men to be executed and others to be imprisoned. The best artillery expert in Russia was Nikolai Voronav. He was in solitary confinement because secret police (NKVD) head Beria did not like his views on heavy artillery. Once released, he led the effort to produce more heavy artillery. General Konstantin Rokossovsky wore metal teeth after his natural teeth had been knocked out during an NKVD questioning. He fought well in Marshal Georgi Zhukov's command.

As for equipment, the Russians fought with some of the most primitive tools as well as some of the most modern. They still used Cossacks fighting on horseback; the horses still moved at -20°F and did not get bogged down in mud or sand. Reindeer sleds carried shells to aircraft in the arctic regions, and dog sleds took extra supplies for infantry. On the other hand, T–34 tanks were better adapted to Russian mud and snow and ran circles around *Panzers*, and the Yak–1M fighter plane equalled the ME–109s in combat.

In Russia war was a matter of timing. Fall and spring rains turned the roads into mud, and winter temperatures dropped to -50° and -60°F. Years of living in this rugged climate conditioned the Russian soldier, and his uniform was made to withstand the cold. Hitler expected his troops to be warmly quartered in Moscow and Leningrad when winter came. By November 7, 1941, Nazi troops were 15 miles away from Moscow. Zhukov mobilized Moscow's population; 250,000 people went to work digging antitank ditches. The defenses

37

held, thanks to fresh troops from Siberia and new weapons from Russian and American factories.

On December 5 the Russians counterattacked, and by Christmas they had driven the Germans back a safe distance from Moscow. Hitler blamed his generals for the failure, and many, from Field Marshal Karl von Rundstedt on down, were transferred or dismissed. The führer decided to take charge personally. Despite complaints of failure from Berlin, the German army had seized 42 percent of Russia's cultivated land and nearly two-thirds of its industrial capacity.

But the Russia of 1942 was far different from that of 1917 when it had meekly retired after being defeated during World War I. Nazi atrocities on the civilian population of the conquered regions made surrender unthinkable. Not all Russian heroes were in the army. Behind German lines guerrilla bands ambushed German supply convoys. Waiting until tanks and trucks carrying soldiers passed by, the guerrillas pounced on the supply and ammunition trucks. There were three million starving people in Leningrad who refused to surrender. Deaths there during the siege numbered 640,000, and the survivors were more dead than alive. For three years the city was within gun range of the invaders. In Moscow those who had not been evacuated lived in unheated apartments and lined up for bread made of flour and sawdust.

About 1,500 factories were boxed up and shipped east, safely beyond Luftwaffe attack. With most men in the 16–40 age group in the army, factories were run by the elderly, children, and women workers. Boys 14–16 years old worked in steel mills on 10-, 12-, or 14-hour shifts. To get them to these new locations workers were put in unheated boxcars. It might take weeks for them to reach their destination. When the boxcars were opened, many were found frozen to death.

Some factories opened before a building was built to cover them, and a building to cover the factory often preceded construction of the barracks for the workers. Resuming production was more important than comfort. Ten weeks after the heavy tank factory at Leningrad was moved out by rail, the relocated factory in the Ural Mountains put out 25 new T–34 tanks.

The effort paid off. In 1942 Russian factories put out 14,300 more tanks, 10,700 more planes, and 21,000 more heavy guns than the Nazis. These facts would make the 1942–1943 battle year a nightmare for the Wehrmacht and their führer.

Debate

The German drive into Russia in 1941–42 was doomed to failure.

Name_____ Date _____

POINTS TO CONSIDER

1. If you had been Hitler, how would you have tried to weaken Russian morale?

_____

_____

_____

_____

_____

2. Do you think Hitler's failure to win in 1941 could be blamed on weather?

_____

_____

_____

_____

_____

3. What sacrifices did Russian civilians make in the war? Do you think Americans would have been equally willing under the circumstances?

_____

_____

_____

_____

_____

Name_____ Date _____

CHALLENGES

1. How did Hitler want the Russian people to be treated?

_____

_____

2. Why did Russian military officers have to be careful about their decisions?

_____

_____

3. How did Voronav get into trouble?

_____

_____

4. How did Rokossovsky lose his teeth?

_____

_____

5. What were three animals used by the Russians?

_____

6. What tanks and what planes did the Russians rely on?

_____

7. What was the closest the Wehrmacht came to Moscow?

_____

8. What part of German truck convoys did guerrillas like to attack?

_____

_____

9. What groups did most of the work in the Russian factories?

_____

_____

10. How many more planes and tanks did the Russians produce than the Nazis did in 1942?

_____

THE NAZI NIGHTMARE AT STALINGRAD

As Hitler and Stalin tried to outguess each other during the winter of 1942, it was the führer who had the upper hand; he could strike for Moscow (the capital), finish off Leningrad (the old czarist capital), or be practical and hit the Russians where they least expected. As he looked at the maps, his eyes kept falling on Stalingrad. That city of 500,000 was important for itself—it cranked out tanks,

The Germans suffered 300,000 casualties during the five-month siege of Stalingrad.

steel, and small arms. It also lay at a key point on the Volga River, and beyond it were the Baku oil fields that kept the Russian war machine supplied. It made sense from a strategic viewpoint. The name also tempted him—capture the city named in honor of his archenemy. Stalingrad was to become the battle on which success or defeat hinged. Hitler vowed: "I'm not going to leave the Volga," and Stalin warned: "Not one step backward. The Volga has now only one bank."

Any military campaign depends in large measure on its leader, and the men picked for Operation Blue were Field Marshal Fritz Manstein and General Friedrich Paulus. Manstein's army was to drive into the Caucasus, and Paulus was to capture Stalingrad. Manstein was a very capable leader who had designed the invasion of France and the attack on Leningrad. Now he was shifted to south Russia for the purpose of taking Sebastapol.

Manstein's attack began May 8 and progressed well at first. By early June he had captured 239,000 prisoners and destroyed over 1,200 tanks. As the Nazi army got close to Sebastapol, however, it met strong resistance. Sebastapol's defenders withstood brutal air and tank attacks. A writer recorded the scene: "There is no town left. The houses are all roofless, the streets are nearly all blocked by avalanches of rubble." The defenders moved into caves, cellars, and dugouts. The siege there lasted 250 days and deprived the *Wehrmacht* of men it needed at Stalingrad.

Paulus was chosen for the Stalingrad assignment because Rundstedt had fallen into disfavor after failing to take Moscow, and Reichinau, under whom Paulus had served, had died in a plane crash. Paulus had never commanded an army before, but he believed Hitler was a military genius, and in Hitler's eyes that qualified him. Paulus developed an attack plan which, if successful, would capture Stalingrad in one week. Only Russian determination stood in his way. Defending the city were generals like Zhukov, Rokossovsky, Yeremenko, Chuikov, and Commissar Nikita Khruschev.

The attack began August 23, and by the next evening Paulus's troops were in Stalingrad. But resistance was strong. There was a lull until fresh German troops could be sent up; then from September 13 on, the two sides battled in a city that was rapidly becoming a giant pile

41

of rubble and twisted metal. A German described Stalingrad as a "cloud of burning, blinding smoke." Chuikov said that the sounds of bullets, shells, and explosions all mingled together into a deafening roar.

The combat in the city was one heroic struggle after another. Small groups of Russians fought until there was no ammunition and no hope. Streets were cleared of Soviet snipers by day, but during the night they moved silently through the streets and sewers to be in position to shoot Nazis on the same street the next day. German air attacks made little difference since their bombs only created more rubble for the Russians to hide behind. A German colonel was amazed by the Soviet infantryman. Disregarding his dead comrades and "without so much as a blink, he stolidly continues the attack."

On November 19 during rain, snow, and freezing rain, the Russians began a counter-attack northwest and south of Stalingrad, hitting hard at the Romanian troops of the Third and Fourth Armies. Poorly equipped and terrified by the attack, their lines collapsed. Paulus realized how dangerous his position was and asked permission to pull back on the next day, but Hitler decreed he must hold the front at all costs. Hitler told him that supplies were coming by air. It wasn't until five days later that Hitler discussed the airlift with Göring, who assured the führer that he could deliver all the supplies they needed by air. Without checking whether he had enough planes or decent landing fields for those planes or noting the impossible flying weather of the region, Göring had made a promise that no one could carry out. Instead of the 500 tons per day required, by December 9 only 84.4 tons were delivered, about 20 percent of what Paulus's starving troops needed. Reduced to catching rats for food, they were no longer an army.

Manstein pled with Hitler to let Paulus try to escape the death trap he was in, but Hitler refused, and Paulus, loyal to the end, did not dare disobey orders. On January 30, 1943, Hitler sent a radio message to Paulus that he had been promoted to the rank of field marshal and reminded him that no German field marshal had ever been taken prisoner. The next day Paulus surrendered. The Germans suffered 300,000 casualties at Stalingrad. Hitler was furious that Paulus surrendered rather than kill himself. "Life is the nation; the individual must die. What remains alive beyond the individual is the nation." Hitler now spent most of his time in his simple quarters at Rastenburg, East Prussia, brooding over maps and withdrawing into a fantasy world.

Debate

Was the outcome at Stalingrad due more to Hitler's mistakes, or the determination of its defenders?

Name _____ Date _____

POINTS TO CONSIDER

1. Did Hitler make a good decision in attacking Stalingrad and Sebastapol rather than Moscow?

_____

_____

_____

_____

_____

2. How did Hitler let down his army at Stalingrad?

_____

_____

_____

_____

_____

3. What do you think the defenses at Stalingrad and Sebastapol told about the Russians as fighters?

_____

_____

_____

_____

_____

Name _____ Date _____

CHALLENGES

1. What was produced at Stalingrad that made it an important target?

_____

2. Who were the commanders of Operation Blue?

_____

3. Why was the siege of Sebastapol important to what happened at Stalingrad?

_____

_____

4. Why was Rundstedt in disfavor at the time of Operation Blue?

_____

5. Name the five Russian leaders who played a big part in what happened at Stalingrad.

_____

_____

6. Why was the *Luftwaffe* of little help over Stalingrad?

_____

_____

7. Who said that he would supply German troops at Stalingrad?

_____

8. Who tried to persuade Hitler to let Paulus withdraw?

_____

9. What was the highest rank Paulus achieved?

_____

10. How many casualties did the Germans suffer at Stalingrad?

_____

THE AFRIKA KORPS REACHES EL ALAMEIN

British Crusader tanks pursue Rommel's defeated troops after the battle at El Alamein.

While some German troops faced -50°F temperatures on the Russian front, others baked in the deserts of North Africa. The struggle for Africa had begun about 1880 and had led to French-German conflicts in Morocco in 1905 and 1911. During World War II, German colonies in east Africa (Tanzania) and southwest Africa (Namibia) were taken by the British. The Italian colonies were Libya on the north coast, and Ethiopia and Somalia in east Africa. In January 1941 British colonial troops from Nigeria and India attacked Ethiopia from the north and in February from the south. In May Haile Selassie took control in Ethiopia. The Italians lost 289,000 men in their struggle to keep their colonies.

Between Italian-held Libya and British-controlled Egypt lay a vast area of the Sahara Desert, hot, sandy, and dry, miserable for men and machines fighting a modern war. To hold so vast an area, more troops were sent in, mostly from New Zealand, Australia, and India. Strengthened with new antitank guns, RAF squadrons, and British and American-made tanks, the British had the advantage.

Another British edge was obvious early in the fighting: the dislike of Italian troops for Mussolini and fascism. As soon as a machine gun opened up or a tank came to the edge of an Italian camp, white flags appeared. When the British needed to build a defensive line, Italian prisoners grabbed shovels and helped. The British moved on to Tobruk, a major port on the Mediterranean. While the British prepared to cut through Italian defenses there, another battle occurred.

Malta lies 60 miles south of Sicily; as a British outpost in the Mediterranean, it was a key to the British supply line across the sea and a menace to the Italian supply line across to Libya. A British convoy moving eastward from Gibraltar in January 1941 was attacked by JU-88s, and the carrier *Illustrious* was crippled. This began air attacks on Malta. Over 1,600 *Luftwaffe* attacks were made on the island during the war. Deep caves were dug in the limestone, and when air raid sirens went off, the civilians, goats, and donkeys calmly headed for the caves. RAF planes were also safely housed in the caves. The island was the home port for the submarines that jeopardized German and Italian supply lines to Africa.

Tobruk fell in January 1941. By February 1941 there was little resistance left to the British. Then two things happened. British troops were taken from North Africa to fight in Greece, and Hitler sent *Panzer* divisions to Africa. In command of this newly formed Afrika Korps was Erwin Rommel who found the desert ideal for his hard-hitting style of fighting.

Rommel had led Panzers into Poland and France, but he became a legend with his Afrika Korps. He was a careful planner who conditioned his men before they were sent to Africa

45

by housing them in overheated barracks, giving them very little water, and kicking up artificial sandstorms with large fans. In Africa he saw that his men were well fed and provided rest areas for them to relax in comfort between campaigns. Rommel was hard on himself and often took personal risks by moving along the front line at night to study enemy gun emplacements. He was so successful and highly respected that he was nicknamed the "Desert Fox."

Commander of the British Eighth Army, General Sir Claude Auchinleck, had set up strong defenses at El Alamein, only 50 miles west of Alexandria and the Nile River. Beyond the Nile lay the oil fields of the Middle East. In the summer of 1942 two new generals were sent to replace Auchinleck: General Sir Harold Alexander (in overall command) and General Sir Bernard Montgomery. The two worked very well together, but "Monty" was the one receiving the fame. The son of an Anglican bishop, he did not smoke, drink, or swear. A perfectionist, he allowed no smoking and only two minutes for coughing at staff meetings. He expected officers to run at least seven miles a week, but after older officers complained, he lowered it to six miles a week.

Monty, like Rommel, preferred inspecting the line in person, and his knowledge of enemy positions was often superior to that of commanders in the sector. He was flamboyant and conceited, but very successful.

Rommel's first effort to recapture Tobruk began with a six-month siege in 1941, but he left in December under pressure from a British offensive. After defeating the British at Gazala in June 1942, he returned to attack Tobruk. Luring the British out to attack him, he destroyed their tanks with his 88-millimeter antitank guns. This time Tobruk surrendered in one day.

El Alamein was a far different battle. Along the 40-mile line both sides had planted thousands of land mines that were barely covered by sand. The British had time to build permanent fortifications along their line. Sappers (specialists in laying and disarming mines) invaded each other's mine fields and neutralized as many as possible, but more were planted the next day. Both sides knew that tanks alone would not win; infantry, artillery, and air support were critical to victory. For two weeks before the battle, the RAF concentrated on destroying Luftwaffe landing fields.

From October 23 to November 4 the critical battle of El Alamein was fought, with the British possessing the better weapons. Rommel had 540 tanks, 280 of them old Italian models; the British had 1,200 tanks, including U.S.-built Grants and Shermans. By November 4 Rommel only had about 80 tanks left. He broke off the battle and pulled back to Tripolitania. Two days later an Allied invasion in west Africa had the Afrika Korps caught in a vise.

Debate

An army should not attack a well-fortified position without overwhelming fire power. No qualities of generalship can change that.

46

Name_____ Date _____

POINTS TO CONSIDER

1. Why was North Africa considered important by both sides in the war?

_____

_____

_____

_____

_____

2. How were Rommel and Montgomery alike in the way they worked?

_____

_____

_____

_____

_____

3. Why do some generals who lose battles still keep a good reputation?

_____

_____

_____

_____

_____

Name_____ Date _____

CHALLENGES

1. What Italian colony was liberated by the British in 1941?

_____

2. What sea was Tobruk on?

_____

3. How many air raids did the Luftwaffe make on Malta?

_____

4. How did the Maltese survive these attacks?

_____

_____

5. What was the German army that was sent to Africa called?

_____

6. How did Rommel train his men to fight in the desert?

_____

_____

7. What was Rommel's nickname?

_____

8. How did Montgomery keep his officers in shape?

_____

_____

9. What is a sapper?

_____

_____

10. Which army had the most tanks at El Alamein?

_____

A "TORCH" LIGHTS IN NORTH AFRICA

In 1942 the war was at a point where it could tilt either way. The Japanese winning streak in the Pacific was not stopped until 1942's battles: the Coral Sea, Midway, and Guadalcanal. In Europe Stalingrad became the big question mark. U.S. and British excuses for not opening a second front (invasion of France) angered Stalin, who suspected the reason for delay was so that more Russians and Germans could kill each other, making the world safe for capitalism. Meeting with Roosevelt in June 1942, Churchill argued that a second front was not yet possible but that an invasion of northwest Africa would re-

Early in the war, western North Africa was controlled by the Nazis through their allies, the Vichy French.

lieve pressure on El Alamein. A British attack plan had already been developed, Operation Super-Gymnast.

Most of western North Africa was ruled by Vichy France, which had promised Hitler it would prevent any landings there. England and Vichy were enemies, but oddly enough, the United States and Vichy still had diplomatic relations. U.S. Ambassador Robert Murphy used his diplomatic status to secretly locate pro-Ally Vichy French officers willing to switch sides if the opportunity came. This U.S. tie to Vichy France infuriated Charles de Gaulle. General of the small Free French army, De Gaulle saw himself as the future leader of liberated France. Roosevelt did not like de Gaulle and ignored his protests.

The new name for the North African invasion was Operation Torch. Placed in command was Lieutenant General Dwight "Ike" Eisenhower. As head of the War Plans Division, he had designed a 1943 invasion of Europe and was respected by General George Marshall. Eisenhower and General Mark Clark had been sent to discuss those plans with Churchill. Those discussions went so well that he was chosen over higher-ranking officers to lead a joint U.S.–British operation in North Africa.

Success of the invasion depended on four things: proper preparation, surprise, sufficient equipment and manpower, and the support of the Vichy French commanders in Morocco and Algeria where landings were to take place. Preparing for a secret operation included details like providing each soldier with his own water purifier, salt tablets, winter underwear for the mountains, and goggles to keep the dust and sun out of his eyes. To prevent problems with the Vichy French, de Gaulle was left in England.

Ambassador Murphy succeeded in finding anti-Nazi French officers in North Africa, and General Clark was sent on a daring submarine mission to meet them. Their talks in an isolated farm house were interrupted by a police patrol looking for smugglers, and Clark hid in the cellar until they left. The information and contacts he gained were very helpful later.

Locations for the attack were Casablanca on the west coast and Algiers and Oran on the north coast. All troop landings were at exactly the same time, 1:00 A.M., on November 8. About 100,000 French troops were stationed in Africa, and these were the first troops the landing forces faced. The only person they listened to was their commander in chief, Admiral Jean Darlan, who happened to be in Algiers visiting his sick son. On November 10 Clark persuaded Darlan to order a cease fire, thus giving the Allies Oran and Casablanca.

Eisenhower was criticized by the British and many Americans for dealing with Darlan, but he felt the circumstances justified his decision. When Darlan was killed by an anti-Nazi Frenchman, he was replaced by General Henri Giraud, a former POW of the Germans who had escaped and been transported to Algiers on a British submarine.

The German reaction to what they viewed as treachery was to move troops into southern France and Tunisia. Rommel moved his army westward with Montgomery's Eighth Army following at a safe distance. Eisenhower had a great deal of work to do. He shifted between being soldier, politician, statesman, and diplomat. He found Air Marshal Sir Arthur Tedder useful in using air power to support land forces. Other problems remained. The Americans, British, and French bickered constantly. Eisenhower had trouble focusing on his military problems.

Rommel surprised his enemies with a stunning victory over a much larger American tank force at Kasserine Pass in western Tunisia on February 19, 1943. Rommel's plan to turn and strike a surprise attack on the Eighth Army failed when Montgomery rushed enough forces to blunt the attack. An important change in command was made after the battle when General George Patton was given command of II Corps. Patton was eccentric, very spit and polish, and as much feared and hated by many of his men as Rommel, but Patton knew how to use tanks and win battles.

The Germans and Italians held on for three more months, but the fate of the Afrika Korps was sealed. Rommel was called back to Berlin in March 1943. His army of 275,000 German and Italian troops surrendered in May. The desert gave valuable combat experience to those who were moving on to fight in Europe. It also taught the need for teamwork if different armies were to achieve success in the long war that lay ahead.

Debate

After the war, the question came up of what to do with Nazi civilian officials in Germany. Some said that if they knew how to do the job better than anyone else, they should be left in charge. Others said that all Nazis were bad and should be removed. Darlan had worked closely with the Germans and apparently approved of their anti-Jewish policies. Was Eisenhower right in working with Darlan as a war necessity?

50

Name_____ Date _____

POINTS TO CONSIDER

1. As Eisenhower's advisor, what would you recommend that might help keep the Germans from knowing where and when you were going to land?

_____

_____

_____

_____

2. If you were preparing an invasion of North Africa, what kinds of things would you be concerned about with respect to your tanks and trucks?

_____

_____

_____

_____

3. Few American troops had any combat experience. What do you think they learned in battle that could not be taught in even the best training?

_____

_____

_____

_____

Name _____ Date _____

CHALLENGES

1. Whom did Churchill think a North African invasion would help?

_____

2. What was the relationship of the United States to Vichy France?

_____

_____

3. Who was Charles de Gaulle?

_____

_____

4. How did Robert Murphy help?

_____

_____

5. What happened to Mark Clark when he went on his secret mission?

_____

_____

6. Who was Jean Darlan?

_____

7. Who replaced Darlan?

_____

8. What country was Tedder from? How did he help Eisenhower?

_____

_____

9. What tank battle in North Africa embarrassed the United States?

_____

10. Where was Rommel when the Afrika Korps surrendered? How many men did Italy and Germany lose in that surrender?

_____

_____

THE ARSENAL FOR DEMOCRACY

The U.S. economy had been weak since the stock market crash in 1929 and the Great Depression that followed. When World War II broke out in Europe, large defense orders came from Great Britain and France, and there was a surge of activity in American industry. As the

Private industry converted to wartime production to supply the Allies with planes, ships, ammunition, and other necessities.

situation in Europe worsened and Japan's expansion threatened Asia, the United States government placed orders for defense related ships, arms, and planes. In his radio "fireside chat" on December 29, 1940, Roosevelt said the United States must be the "arsenal for democracy." By this he meant that U.S. factories must produce the arms, ships, and planes that would help the United States and its allies. Already, the nation was feeling the economic benefits of war production.

Many Americans, however, feared that the war might destroy the democracy the nation was fighting for. Fascism and communism showed that powerful government takes away freedoms. Others remembered the agencies created by the United States during World War I to control food, production, railroads, labor relations, and public opinion. With the New Deal agencies already so powerful, conservatives feared a major war might ruin the American free enterprise system and lead to dictatorship.

As the United States geared up for war, it was with a different philosophy than existed in most countries. (1) The American free enterprise system was to be protected. Secretary of War Henry Stimson said: "If you are going to try to go to war in a capitalist country, you have got to let business make money out of the process or business won't work." (2) Civilian goods were limited because of military needs, but civilian needs were met. Some parts of traditional American life like baseball, Broadway plays, and movie production continued. Quality suffered, but sports and recreation were considered important. (3) Plenty of work was available, and most workers were free to move from one employer to another. (4) Unlike Axis countries, Americans inside and outside government were free to criticize red tape, inefficiency, incompetence, waste, and corruption.

Many government agencies were created to handle the war effort, but just a few will be mentioned. The War Production Board (WPB) was headed by Donald Nelson. Its basic jobs were to (1) stop production of many civilian goods using steel and iron and (2) set up a priority system directing raw materials and products to companies and consumers.

The Office of Price Administration (OPA) was headed by Leon Henderson. Its job was to hold down inflation by setting wages, regulating rent, and setting prices for basic goods and services. To keep any consumer from buying more than he needed, ration books were issued beginning in the spring of 1942. Among items rationed during the war were meat (beef, pork, and poultry), shoes, sugar, cheese, and gasoline. Henderson knew he was going to be unpopular, and he often angered labor leaders, farmers, landlords, and Americans unhappy over rationing. Gas rationing was needed because of the rubber shortage. A person with an "A" sticker could buy only three gallons a week. Despite the complaints, from September 1942 to August 1945 the cost of living rose only 29 percent.

Everyone knew about the WPB and OPA, but an important, little-noticed agency was the Office of Scientific Research and Development (OSRD). Its 6,000 scientists were led by Vannevar Bush and worked without publicity or the possibility of receiving patents. Among their developments were improvements in radar, sonar, explosives, and missiles. Their products included fireproof clothing, night vision equipment, self-steering torpedoes, and the Duck (a truck running on either land or water).

To become the "arsenal for democracy" required a number of changes. Ships and planes had to be built by newer and faster techniques. Aircraft manufacturing became assembly line production. In 1939 the United States built 5,856 planes; in 1940, 26,277; in 1942, 47,836; in 1943, 85,898; and in 1944, 96,318. Ford Motor Company put out B-25s at a Willow Run, Michigan, plant that was a half-mile long. Henry Kaiser's ship plants used mass production techniques as well. His first cargo vessel took 197 days to build; in 1944, one was built in 14 days. Reynolds Aluminum alone produced more aluminum than did the United States, England, and France in 1939. Large companies often contracted with smaller companies for parts. Cooperation like that in World War II had never been seen before in American industry.

Production was needed in many other areas as well. General Brehon Somervell, who was in charge of supplying forces' needs, said that his Armed Service Forces (ASF) purchase list for 1943 alone included 9,500 light and medium tanks, 21,000 boxcars, 7 million packages of gauze, 17 million neckties, and 60 million pairs of socks. Products that could fill more than one need were developed. A new soap came out that could work in any kind of water, made shaving lather, and could be used as toothpaste.

Job opportunities opened for many groups. White collar workers sometimes worked a half shift after an eight-hour day at the office. Older people rejoined the work force. A Dodge plant created an Old Men's Department that did lighter production work. The supervisor was 77 years old, the average age was 66. In efficiency and quality, they performed better than the plant average. Women took jobs that had always been labeled "men's work," and minorities found that the shortage of workers finally made it possible for them to be employed in defense industries.

Debate in 1942

Is America as we have always known it gone forever?

Name_____ Date _____

POINTS TO CONSIDER

1. War is seen by most people as tragic, but to Americans in 1941 it was not so bad. Why did they feel that way, and why was their opinion somewhat different in 1942?

_____

_____

_____

_____

2. List ten civilian items that would not be produced if the WPB were needed again.

_____

_____

_____

_____

3. Why were price controls seen as important during World War II?

_____

_____

_____

_____

Name_____ Date _____

CHALLENGES

1. Who coined the phrase "arsenal for democracy"?

_____

2. What happened during World War I that caused people to worry about big government?

_____

_____

3. Who said that business should be allowed to make money?

_____

4. What were three parts of traditional life not interfered with?

_____

_____

5. Which agency stopped production of civilian cars?

_____

6. Which government agency limited the civilian purchase of gasoline?

_____

7. What were some groups who were unhappy with Leon Henderson?

_____

_____

8. What agency developed fireproof clothing?

_____

9. How many more planes were produced in 1944 than in 1939?

_____

10. What was the fastest that Henry Kaiser's plant could build a ship?

_____

AMERICAN WOMEN IN THE WAR

When World War II began, many men and women took the traditional view that "a woman's place is in the home," but war needs had vetoed tradition before and they were going to do it again. In the Civil War women worked as clerks, nurses, and even spies. World War I women were used as telephone operators by the Army Signal Corps or as "yeomanette" clerks in the Navy Department. They also worked in defense industries or in volunteer agencies.

World War II was an even bigger war, and every woman had a husband, son, father, or friend in the armed services. The women wanted to help, and eventually they were doing almost everything except combat duty for their nation. Often ignored or unfairly criticized, they worked long hours, sometimes in dangerous industrial and military jobs.

It was not easy to persuade women to take industrial jobs. Few women had ever worked in a factory, but when "Rosie the Riveter," symbol of this new breed of woman, flexed her muscles, they went to the nearby aircraft assembly plant or shipyard and applied. There were many problems faced by women working in World War II defense

Those who served in the Women's Army Corps performed clerical work, parachute rigging, glider instruction, and other valuable tasks.

plants that today's woman does not face. (1) Women always wore dresses then, and it was hard to feel feminine or proper in the jeans and coveralls required at work. (2) Housework was very time consuming. There were no microwaves, dishwashers, automatic washing machines and driers, or fast food chains. After hours at work, washing and ironing awaited them at home. (3) The gas shortage made it difficult to get to work, so women wondered if it was acceptable to hitchhike. Emily Post said it was permissable for a lady to hitchhike, but she should use her work badge and not her thumb to signal for a ride. (4) If she had children, a babysitter was needed. Sometimes grandma was available, but often grandma was working too. (5) Male supervisors and co-workers gave them a hard time.

At aircraft assembly plants, women were not accepted at first, but after some experimental hirings at a few factories, many began hiring them. Most plants paid them the usual 60¢ an hour starting wage, but some hired college girls at 75¢ an hour. After a few months with women workers, plant managers said they could run the factory with somewhere between 50 and 85 percent women. By the end of the war, four million women were employed at defense plants. Women knew that these jobs were not permanent and did not expect to be employed in them after the men returned from the war. Still, it was a good learning experience, and it gave many women a feeling of independence they had never had before.

For women whose circumstances did not permit them to do work outside the home, there were many volunteer jobs they could take. The American Women's Voluntary Services (AWVS) organized courses in auto repair and switchboard operations. They also started salvage drives and prepared surgical dressings. The Office of Civil Defense (OCD) trained women as air raid wardens. The American Red Cross (ARC) provided many kinds of services to men in uniform. The United Services Organization (USO) provided doughnuts and coffee at railroad stations for troop trains and set up dances and entertainment for men in nearby military bases. Women's groups in churches had prayer vigils, sent newspaper clippings, and wrote letters to local servicemen. Families used valuable ration stamps to provide a homecooked Sunday dinner for total strangers in uniform.

All three services used women in uniform. The army version was the Women's Auxiliary Army Corps (WAAC—later the "Auxiliary" was dropped, and the corps became known as the WACs). By 1943 there were 150,000 WACs, and in 1945, 15,500 were serving overseas. Commanded by Major Oveta Culp Hobby, the types of jobs performed by WACs included clerical work, processing blood tests, parachute rigging, and glider instruction.

WAVES were commanded by Captain Mildred McAfee, and they were the navy's version of WACs. Their assignments were often the same as WACs, but they also became meteorologists and repaired airplanes. Lieutenant Colonel Ruth Streeter commanded the women marines, often called "Lady Leathernecks." Their work included painting airplanes, electrical work, cooking, and shoe repair. Coast Guard women were called SPARS.

England had women pilots, but in the United States many army officers were reluctant to use them because they were "too high strung." As often happened during the war, practical needs overcame prejudice. General Henry (Hap) Arnold, who headed the army air force, gave approval in 1942 for women to ferry planes from aircraft factories to bases and from one base to another. Some women selected were already licensed pilots, but others had to be trained. Called the WASPs (Women Airforce Service Pilots), they eventually flew 77 types of planes, including B–24s and B–25s.

Eleanor Roosevelt wrote: "Undoubtedly, there are some women who are leading the same sort of life today that they have always led; but I think they must be having a difficult time finding companionship. For the vast majority of women in this country, life has changed. They are only content if they feel they are contributing something toward the speedier ending of the war and a better chance for their particular men in the world of the future."

Debate in 1942

Some groups are saying that creating the WACs is going to take the woman away from her traditional role as housewife and mother. Do you agree?

Name_____ Date _____

POINTS TO CONSIDER

1. How difficult was it for women to take jobs in defense plants?

_____

_____

_____

_____

_____

2. Why was volunteer involvement so important during the war? To what extent do people volunteer today?

_____

_____

_____

_____

_____

3. What skills did women gain in the war that gave them more independence after the war?

_____

_____

_____

_____

_____

Name_____ Date _____

CHALLENGES

1. In what war did women first work as clerks and spies?

_____

2. What were women navy clerks called in World War I?

_____

3. What did Emily Post say about women hitchhiking?

_____

_____

4. What was the usual starting wage?

_____

5. What group taught women how to repair their own cars?

_____

6. What group provided entertainment for servicemen?

_____

7. What were women in the army called?

_____

8. What were women in the navy called?

_____

9. What excuse did air force officers give for not using women pilots?

_____

_____

10. How did Eleanor Roosevelt feel women had changed?

_____

_____

AMERICA'S MINORITIES IN THE WAR

Race relations in the United States were not good when the war began. There was much prejudice and discrimination against "people of color," and some in these groups wondered why they should fight the "white man's war." However, the Nazi racial views and the Japanese treatment of conquered nations made it clear to most minority groups that this was their war too. As boxing champion Joe Louis put it: "America's got lots of problems, but Hitler won't fix them." Minority members knew most Americans looked down on them, so they wanted to prove worthy of equal treatment after the war was over.

Many black troops were recognized for bravery and valor during the war. Minority soldiers began to gain the respect of the white soldiers they served with.

BLACKS (the preferred term of the time) lived in the South or in urban ghettos in the North when the war began, but job opportunities and military service scattered them much more than ever before. In the army blacks served in segregated units, usually under white officers. In 1942 ROTC training programs began at black colleges to train officers, and a flying school for black aviators was started at Tuskegee, Alabama. By the end of the war, over 80 black pilots had won the Distinguished Flying Cross. About 4,000 black women were in the WACs. The navy had only used blacks as cooks and servants before the war, but in 1942 they began training blacks for regular sea duty. A special training base for black sailors was established at the Great Lakes Training Center.

The Marines were slow to admit blacks, but after finding them as good as any men in their uniform, the Corps commander pronounced: "Negro Marines are no longer on trial. They are Marines, period." Blacks in the army were often in labor batallions, but some became engaged in heavy fighting. The 761st Tank Battalion was in the thick of the Battle of the Bulge, and the 614th Tank Destroyer Battalion fought in many battles. The Ninety-ninth Air Squadron shot down eight German planes in one day.

When the war began, few defense plants hired blacks, and in 1942 A. Philip Randolph, a black union leader, pressured Roosevelt into signing Executive Order 8802. It required that there be no discrimination in employment of defense workers "because of race, creed, color, or national origin." The Fair Employment Practices Commission (FEPC) was to investigate violations of this order. Still, discrimination continued.

MEXICANS who came across the border to take farm labor jobs were often badly treated, and the FEPC began looking into discrimination. The State Department objected because they feared Latin American nations would turn against the United States. Relations between Mexicans and whites were especially tense in California where those of Mexican ancestry were barred from certain public places. Still, many Mexican-Americans served their nation well during the war.

There were about 600,000 Italian citizens living in America and five million *ITALIAN-AMERICANS* at the beginning of the war. Many of these admired Mussolini before the United States entered the war, but their attitudes changed quickly after Pearl Harbor. The government clamped down on Italians and Germans who were not citizens. They could not travel without permission or own shortwave radios, maps, or guns. These restrictions were lifted in 1942.

Many Americans along the West Coast had long been hostile to the "yellow peril" and used the attack on Pearl Harbor as an excuse to punish their *JAPANESE-AMERICAN* population. Three generations of Japanese descent were in America: *Issei* (those born in Japan), *Nisei* (first generation native-born Americans), and *Sansei* (second generation native-born). To General John DeWitt, commander of West Coast defense, it made no difference whether he was an American citizen or not: "A Jap is a Jap." In the days following Pearl Harbor, over 2,000 Japanese were rounded up, many on ridiculous charges. In January 1942 security zones were established on the West Coast from which enemy aliens were to be removed.

In February 1942 President Roosevelt issued Executive Order 9066, which authorized relocation camps. All Japanese-Americans, even if they had sons in the U.S. Army or Navy, were to be sent to camps in seven western states. They were to report to an assembly center, usually a fairground or race track without proper sanitation. Barracks were built for them in barren and isolated locations. One camp in Utah was on a salt flat where the temperature was 130°F in summer, -30°F in winter.

Some of the relocated joined the army, and after training in Wisconsin, fought valiantly in the Italian campaign. A few protested in court against this violation of their rights. Fred Koramatsu refused to report for relocation and appealed to the U.S. Supreme Court. Justice Black wrote the majority decision. He wrote that he had no reason to doubt the loyalty of most Japanese-Americans and that relocation was a hardship for them. But he wrote: "Hardships are part of war, and war is an aggregation of hardships . . . When under conditions of modern warfare our shores are threatened by hostile forces, the power to protect must be [equal] with the threatened danger."

Justice Roberts wrote: "It is the case of convicting a citizen as a punishment for not submitting to imprisonment in a concentration camp, based on his ancestry, and solely because of his ancestry, without evidence or inquiry concerning his loyalty and good disposition toward the United States." Apologies and damage payments would have to wait until after the war.

Debate in 1942

The situation today requires that Japanese on the West Coast should be relocated.

Name_____ Date _____

POINTS TO CONSIDER

1. What were some ways blacks were discriminated against?

_____

_____

_____

_____

_____

2. If you were a Nisei, how would you feel about the way you were being treated in comparison with your German-born neighbor?

_____

_____

_____

_____

_____

3. Do you think General DeWitt was responding the way he did because he felt the Japanese were a threat, or did his actions come from prejudice?

_____

_____

_____

_____

_____

Name _____ Date _____

CHALLENGES

1. Why did Joe Louis think African-Americans should fight?

_____

_____

2. Where were black aviators trained?

_____

3. What were two black battalions that saw a great deal of battle?

_____

4. What kinds of discrimination were covered by Executive Order 8802?

_____

5. Why was the State Department upset over FEPC investigations into the treatment of Mexican-Americans?

_____

_____

6. What restrictions were put on German and Italian citizens?

_____

7. What was the difference between Issei and Nisei Japanese?

_____

_____

8. What was Executive Order 9066?

_____

9. On what basis did Justice Black approve relocation?

_____

_____

10. What questions did Justice Roberts think should have been asked before relocation was required?

_____

_____

LIFE UNDER THE THIRD REICH

When Hitler took power in Germany in 1933, few outside Germany saw him as anything more than just another of those dictators taking advantage of the Depression. His Nazis were brutal, but they were Germany's problem, no one else's. Events from 1936 on proved them wrong.

LEADERS. The Nazi movement was like a giant net scooping up misfits and giving them power. Rudolf Hess was a fanatical Nazi who had been imprisoned with Hitler

The Nazis used propaganda, fear, and a spirit of extreme nationalism to fuel their movement.

after the 1923 putsch failed. By 1939 he was deputy führer. Without Hitler's approval, he flew to Scotland in 1939 to convince England not to fight Germany. He spent the rest of his life in prison.

Hermann Göering was a man of enormous power, wealth, and size. A fighter pilot in World War I, he shot down 22 planes. He became a Nazi in 1923 and was wounded in the putsch. He escaped to Austria where he became a morphine addict. In 1935 he became *Luftwaffe* commander in chief. Air victories gave Göering prestige, and Hitler rewarded him with the title of Reichsmarshall. After air defeats over Britain, his enemies (Himmler, Goebbels, and Bormann) united to undercut his popularity with Hitler.

Joseph Goebbels, minister of propaganda, was the best-educated Nazi leader. He earned his Ph.D. at the University of Heidelberg, but his early efforts to become a writer failed. In 1924 he joined the Nazi Party and became very successful as a speaker, writer, creator of mass rallies, and movie producer. He was a little, crippled man with a wife and six children, but everyone in Germany knew about his affairs with a Czech actress.

Martin Bormann, party minister in charge of party headquarters, was less well known than other leaders, but he was Hitler's right hand man and had the power to decide which officials saw the führer. Bormann kept the jealousy between the other leaders alive and used it to his own advantage.

LIFE IN NAZI GERMANY. The Nazis stressed their Aryan (Nordic) origins. They said that Germans were the "master race." The führer was the leader of the race and deserved total obedience. The party did the work of the führer and so promoted the good of the race. Mass rallies, parades, ceremonies, and shows of military strength overwhelmed critics' protests.

Young people not only went to school, but those between the ages of 10 and 18 were forced to join Hitler youth organizations: HJ and DJ for boys, BDM and JM for girls. Their motto was "Führer command, we follow!" Schools also stressed Nazi teachings. In a math class, one question was: "If it costs 6 million RMs to build an insane asylum, how many houses at 15,000 RMs could have been built for that amount?"

Heinrich Himmler, head of the SS, worried about the number of Aryan men being killed in the war. His SS needed more men, and quickly. To be SS, a man had to prove he was of Aryan stock. When he wanted to marry, his fiance's photograph (with her dressed in a swimming suit) was sent to Himmler; his decision was required. He judged the girl on her Nordic features and on whether or not she would produce strong children.

To increase the supply of German Aryans, Himmler took Polish blue-eyed, blond-haired children from their parents and had them adopted by Germans. In 1939 the Nazis began ridding Germany of deformed children and the insane. The children were slowly starved to death, and the insane were killed in gas chambers. When church leaders learned about these programs, they were stopped, but by that time 90,000 had already been killed.

What did the Germans have in mind for their conquered neighbors? Hitler intended for heavy industries to be moved to Germany; that way, they could never challenge German rule. Germany would use France, Belgium, and Holland to produce agricultural goods, Slovakia and Hungary for cheap textiles, and the Balkan nations for shoes and furniture.

The conquered peoples were expected to give Germany anything it wanted. In Denmark, Germans seized many dairy herds, other livestock, and poultry; these were paid for with German occupation money. The Danes, from King Christian X on down, enjoyed irritating the Germans. A dealer put a sign for a new book in his window: *English in 50 Hours:* LEARN ENGLISH BEFORE THE TOMMIES ARRIVE. The Germans ordered it taken down. The next day, he put up a new sign: *German in 50 Hours:* LEARN GERMAN BEFORE OUR FRIENDS THE GERMANS DEPART. At first the Danes were treated better than most conquered people, but by 1944 Danes were treated the same as the others.

Many Dutch opposed the Germans by helping to hide Jews, joining the resistance movement, or refusing to sign loyalty oaths. Young people who did not sign the required oaths were called *Onderdruikers* (under-divers), and if caught, they and the persons hiding them were shot. The Germans rounded up factory workers and sent them to labor in German industries. French workers were also forced to work for the Nazis. At one factory they were housed in dog kennels only three feet high and had no access to water.

The worst treatment, however, was reserved for Eastern Europeans who, to Nazi eyes, were "subhumans." Polish and Ukrainian property was seized, and many "undesirables" (including gypsies and Jews) were shot. Able-bodied workers were sent to forced labor factories where they worked from 5 A.M. to 6 P.M., living on turnip soup and a few small potatoes a day.

Debate

Was it possible to be a Nazi and a decent human being at the same time?

Name _____ Date _____

POINTS TO CONSIDER

1. What would growing up in Nazi Germany do to the mind of a student?

_____

_____

_____

_____

2. What idea was the math question trying to get across?

_____

_____

_____

_____

3. If you lived in one of the captive countries, how would you try to get even with the Nazis?

_____

_____

_____

_____

Name ———————————————— Date ——————

CHALLENGES

1. What was Rudolf Hess's title before he left Germany?

_____

2. What job did Göering have in the Nazi government?

_____

_____

3. Who handled propaganda for the Nazis?

_____

4. Who decided which persons got in to see Hitler?

_____

5. Why did the Nazis say that Hitler deserved total obedience?

_____

_____

6. What were the Hitler youth organizations for boys called?

_____

7. What happened to Polish children with blue eyes and blond hair?

_____

_____

8. Who did the Germans think would supply Germany with food after the war?

_____

_____

9. How did the Danes try to get even with the Germans?

_____

_____

10. Why were Poles and Ukrainians treated so badly?

_____

_____

THE FINAL SOLUTION SPREADS

The "Final Solution" is a topic that is very difficult for sane people today to understand, and some refuse to believe it ever happened at all. However, the record is complete and cannot be denied: people lost their property, livelihoods, dignity, and lives because they were born Jewish. Hitler did not invent the segregation of the Jews, the ghetto, or the yellow Star of David patches. Abusing Jews was an old custom in many countries including Spain, Germany, Poland, and Russia. Some Jews saw trouble coming and left Germany before the worst came, but others thought it was a passing phase and would go away, just as pogroms (government-approved attacks on Jews) had in Russia under the czars.

Laws restricting the freedom of Jews forced many to leave Germany, but most had nowhere to go and could not escape the persecution.

Hitler never made a secret of his dislike for Jews; he held them responsible for the Treaty of Versailles, the terrible economic conditions of Germany, and almost every catastrophe that had hurt Germany. Yet Jews made up less than 1 percent of the German population, and only in Frankfurt were they more than 4 percent of a city's population. Despite their small numbers, they played a major part in the professions: 16 percent of lawyers, 15 percent of brokers, and 10.9 percent of doctors were Jews.

Shortly after Hitler came to power, the SA enforced a boycott of Jewish shops, accusing them of protesting to outsiders about attacks on synagogues and individuals. Police were instructed not to interfere with the boycott but to become involved only if life or property were threatened. The boycott didn't last long because most Germans did not like it. In April 1933 a law was passed limiting the number of Jewish civil servants and judges, and another law set a quota requiring that Jews could number no more than 5 percent of the students at any school.

In 1935 new laws were passed to (1) forbid marriage between Jews and citizens of German blood; (2) forbid Jews to fly the national flag, although they could fly a Jewish flag; (3) change the status of Jews from citizens to subjects; (4) prohibit Jews from using the library and attending the theatre; and (5) force Jewish men to add "Israel" as a middle name and women to add "Sarah" to theirs. Passports were stamped "Jew." Jews were still somewhat protected by public opinion, and there was confusion among the Nazis over the exact definition of who was a Jew and as to how far back to trace Jewish ancestry.

Because the Olympics were to be held in Berlin in 1936, Hitler feared that continuing his harsh treatment of Jews might cause the games to be moved elsewhere. Pressure on Jews eased until 1938 when a Jew was accused of murdering a minor German Foreign Office official in Paris. In a radio announcement Goebbels told Germans to demonstrate their outrage, and that night, November 10, 1938, mobs broke the windows at Jewish-owned stores and synagogues. So much broken glass was left on the streets that this was called *Kristallnacht* (Crystal Night). The attacks on property and individuals were so savage that no one tried to stop them.

The Jewish question was now at a critical point, and Hitler was impatient with delays in ridding Germany of its Jews. His policies were already working. From 1933 to 1937, 129,000 Jews had left the country, and in 1938, 40,000 more left. On November 12, 1938, Göring announced that after January 1, 1939, Jews could no longer run businesses or be supervisors. Jews were being forced out, but to where? By now, most were very poor and could not afford to move. Other countries did not want them, and the British allowed only a few into Palestine because of Arab complaints.

World War II created a new and bigger Jewish problem for the Nazis because conquered nations like Poland, Russia, France, and the Netherlands were home to thousands of Jews. Even Denmark and Norway had small Jewish populations. In 1941 Hitler proposed the "Final Solution," the death of all Jews in Europe. The SS agency designated to accomplish this was the RSHA, headed by Rienhard Heydrich. He called a meeting of leaders of the departments whose help was needed to accomplish this at the Berlin suburb of Wannsee. With cold efficiency they discussed timetables and methods.

The Jews had many enemies in some countries, and these enemies were more than willing to help SS death squads locate Jews. The Germans often went to Jewish villages in Poland and the Ukraine and said workers were needed. Those chosen sometimes were put on work details or were sent to work as slave labor in a factory, but others were taken into the woods and shot.

Some Christians saw what was happening to the Jews and helped them escape, hid them away, or took Jewish children into their homes and forged papers showing they were the children of relatives who had died in the war. When Nazi officials told Denmark's King Christian X to solve his Jewish problem, he told the Nazis that Denmark did not have a Jewish problem: "We know we are their equals."

Debate in 1938

Taking into consideration that these are Depression years and that there is very high unemployment, debate whether the United States should allow all Jewish refugees to immigrate.

Name _____ Date _____

POINTS TO CONSIDER

1. Why didn't more Jews leave in 1933?

_____

_____

_____

_____

2. At what point do you think life got so bad in Germany that Jews realized their nightmare was only beginning?

_____

_____

_____

_____

_____

3. What could you have done to help a Jewish neighbor and friend during this time?

_____

_____

_____

_____

Name_____ Date _____

CHALLENGES

1. What had the systematic persecution of Jews in Russia been called?

_____

2. What was the most Jewish German city, and what percent of its people were Jews?

_____

3. What three professions had unusually high percentages of Jews?

_____

_____

4. What was the SA excuse for the boycott in 1933?

_____

_____

5. Name two prominent Jews who left Germany in 1933.

_____

6. What names did Jews have to add to their given names in 1935?

_____

7. Why did pressure on Jews let up in 1936?

_____

_____

8. Where did the name "Crystal Night" come from?

_____

_____

9. What was Hitler's "Final Solution" to be?

_____

_____

10. What agency was to carry it out?

_____

THE ISLAND WAR IN THE PACIFIC

Across a semicircle south of Japan lay the Dutch East Indies (Indonesia), New Guinea, and the Solomon Island chain. These islands were important because: (1) the East Indies provided oil to Japan, (2) a complete Japanese victory in New Guinea put Australia within range of air attack and even invasion, and (3) it endangered the U.S. supply line to Australia. The center of Japanese activity in that region was Rabaul on New Britain Island. Well protected by 300 planes, it was considered too strong for ground attack. Instead, the Allies planned to eat away at Japanese strength in the Solomons and New Guinea, inching their

U.S. marines marching through the jungle on Guadalcanal

way toward Rabaul. The "Yanks" and the "Aussies" were going to face some of the worst fighting of the war.

Even though the European war was getting the highest priority of men and supplies, Admiral Ernest King succeeded in getting agreement from higher-ups that no less than 30 percent of combined resources should be aimed against Japan. The U.S. Navy always had at least two-thirds of its strength in the Pacific.

U.S. leaders in the Pacific were an odd combination of personalities. General Douglas MacArthur was a brilliant man who ignored superiors, angered equals, and browbeat subordinates. He served as supreme commander of the Southwest Pacific Area. But armies need transportation and support from the navies. Admiral Chester Nimitz, a Texan, had been picked for naval command in the region because Roosevelt had a "hunch" he was the best man. Likable, pleasant, and calm, Nimitz also played hunches, and at Midway, they paid off in victory. One of his top men was Admiral William (Bull) Halsey whose remarks often made headlines and who won popularity with his men.

During the years between wars, the U.S. Marines were used mostly for jungle wars in Haiti and Nicaragua. When not exercising those responsibilities, the marines practiced amphibious landings and served as guards on ships on Chinese rivers. They knew better than others the toughness of the Japanese soldiers. Their top man was General Alexander Vandergrift.

Those fighting in the South Pacific suffered from the oppressive heat, the stench of decaying vegetation, knee-deep mud, and attacks by scorpions, mosquitoes, and giant leeches. Diseases were almost as deadly as the Japanese who were well dug in on these islands. Two Japanese words described the fighting. *Banzai* (literally "10,000 years," meaning that a man is prepared to die for the emperor) charges were first experienced on Guadalcanal; no quarter was given by the attacking Japanese in these quick charges. *Bushido* was the code requiring that the soldier fight to the death. Suicide was more common

73

than surrender.

GUADALCANAL was the largest island in the Solomons and was the site for the first U.S. offensive in the Pacific, an attack showing the need for cooperation between sea, air, and land forces. The Japanese were building an air base on the island and had to be stopped. The code name for the attack was Operation Watchtower, but the limited resources available gave it the nickname Operation Shoestring. U.S. Marines landed on the island in August 1942, and for the next six months wrestled the Japanese for its control. Japanese supplies kept coming down the "Slot," a 400-mile path between islands to Guadalcanal. The U.S. Navy could clear the Slot by day, but at night ships brought new men and provisions. In November, a Japanese battleship task force joined 11 transports on a delivery run, and an attempt was made to wipe out the air base, renamed Henderson Field. In the naval battle that followed, a Japanese battleship and six transports were sunk.

NEW GUINEA was a very large island with the Japanese in control of the north side and Australian troops defending Port Moresby on its south side. The Japanese advanced toward Port Moresby over the very narrow Kokoda Trail, but stopped 30 miles from the port because their commander needed to send more men to Guadalcanal. They were pushed back north by the Aussies while U.S. forces attempted landings along the coast. MacArthur ordered his men to capture Buna, where the Japanese had built strong defenses. The men landed without flame throwers, tanks, or artillery, and were beaten back. The last Japanese surrendered on New Guinea in September 1945.

North of these islands were those in the Gilberts (including Tarawa), the Marshalls (including Kwajalein), and the Marianas (including Saipan). The tactic used here was called "island hopping"—attacking some islands, but leaving the Japanese on other islands with no supplies coming in and no place to go. On TARAWA, the 5,000-man Japanese garrison fought to the end, and after the last suicide charge in November 1943, there were only 17 survivors. At KWAJALEIN, seven U.S. battleships blasted the 2.5-mile island for three days and killed all senior Japanese officers. Despite that, the Japanese put up a tough fight with the U.S. Army and Marine troops who took the island in January 1944.

When the strongly fortified island of SAIPAN fell in July 1944, the truth about the war finally came clearly to the Japanese people who had not been told the truth about previous defeats. At Saipan, 3,000 Japanese went to their death in a banzai charge, and 8,000 civilians killed themselves by jumping off a ledge into shark-infested waters.

When GUAM was taken, the United States recaptured its first piece of real estate. Again, Japanese resistance was strong, and deep in the jungles, some remained long after the war was over. In 1972 a Japanese soldier, Corporal Yokoi Shoichi, came out of his hiding place to surrender.

Debate in 1943

Which service (the army and army air force or the navy) deserves credit for stopping the Japanese advance in the Pacific?

Name _____ Date _____

POINTS TO CONSIDER

1. Why was it necessary for land, sea, and air forces to work together in the Pacific?

_____

_____

_____

_____

_____

2. Why was fighting in the Pacific harder on the men than fighting in Europe?

_____

_____

_____

_____

_____

3. Why do you think the Japanese soldiers made banzai charges?

_____

_____

_____

_____

_____

Name_____ Date _____

CHALLENGES

1. What continent was in danger because of the Japanese advance southward?

_____

2. What percentage of the total Allied effort was put into the Pacific war?

_____

3. What title did MacArthur have?

_____

4. Who was in charge of the U.S. Navy in the Pacific?

_____

5. Who was the top marine?

_____

6. What was the literal translation of *banzai?* What did the Japanese mean by the word?

_____

_____

7. What was the unofficial name for the Guadalcanal campaign?

_____

8. What was the importance of the Slot?

_____

_____

9. What town in New Guinea were the Japanese trying to capture? How close did they come?

_____

_____

10. How did Japanese civilians react on Saipan after the banzai charge failed?

_____

_____

MARSHALL'S TEAM IN EUROPE

If the U.S. Army in World War II were a professional football team, Roosevelt would have been the owner; General George Marshall, the general manager; and MacArthur and Eisenhower, the head coaches. It was Marshall who made decisions on which coach got how many men and how much equipment and had to explain to the owner and the fans why the war was not proceeding faster and why so many Americans were being killed and injured. The qualities of thick skin, fairness, and good judgment were needed for someone in Marshall's job. Fortunately, he had them.

George Catlett Marshall

General MARSHALL (he was always addressed as "General," even by the president) was a VMI (Virginia Military Institute) man, not a West Pointer. He ruled by example; he kept himself in perfect shape, worked long hours, and never demanded from others what he did not expect from himself. Performance, not praise, was the way to win his approval. He judged his staff by their ability, and even someone as irritating as MacArthur kept his job because he did it well. At times, the press and politicians jumped on players like Patton, and Marshall had to bench them for a while. But if they were high-quality performers, he put them back into the game when they were needed.

General Dwight (Ike) EISENHOWER was a West Pointer. He served in World War I but was never in combat. During the years between the wars, he left the infantry, spent time in the tank corps, and earned aviator wings. He impressed Marshall with his ability and was put in charge of the War Planning Office after Pearl Harbor. His work, personal charm, and diplomatic skills made their impression on both Roosevelt and Churchill. In 1942 he was appointed to command the U.S. forces in Europe (ETOUSA), and then to command Operation Torch, the invasion of North Africa.

To make sure the British and U.S. officers were pulling in the same direction, he put them across from each other in meetings so each army knew exactly what the other was doing. He would not tolerate any U.S. officer who treated the English as inferiors. Sea landings are always difficult to carry out, so he needed not only diplomatic skills but also great organizational ability. He proved he had both time after time.

Eisenhower's Chief of Staff was W. Beadle SMITH, a tough man who had an eye for detail but could also see the big picture. Smith could be diplomatic when the situation required it, but whether it was because of his ulcer or his natural temperament, he was very difficult on his staff. Churchill called him "the American Bulldog." Eisenhower described him as one who "really takes charge of things in a big way. I wish I had a dozen like him."

Working under Eisenhower was his West Point classmate, General Omar BRADLEY.

In Bradley's West Point yearbook, Ike wrote: "True merit is like a river, the deeper it is, the less noise it makes." At the beginning of WWII, Bradley was training troops, and when they went on 25-mile hikes, he marched with them. A journalist wrote of him at the time: "He is not showy enough to become legend . . . The general doesn't only command respect. He wins devotion." Bradley was always polite to his troops, but was no popularity seeker. When the time came for tough decisions, he made them. Ernie Pyle rated Bradley the best general in the war, and the men who served under him regarded him highly.

George PATTON was described by Bradley as "the most fiercely ambitious man and the strangest duck I ever met." Patton won the Distinguished Service Cross for leading his tank corps into battle in WWI. He believed firmly in his tanks, and was convinced that they would help him fulfill his destiny. Before he left the States, Patton visited General John J. Pershing, who had been his commander during the Mexican troubles in 1916. Pershing told him: "I can always pick a fighting man and God knows there are few of them. I am happy they are sending you to the front at once. I like generals so bold they are dangerous. I hope they give you a free hand." Eisenhower and Bradley saw war as a dirty job, but Patton rejoiced in it. Patton had studied history so much that he imagined himself fighting alongside Alexander the Great, Caesar, and Napoleon.

There were two problems that marred Patton's career. (1) He was outspoken in his dislike for Montgomery and the British in general, and Eisenhower often warned him to keep his mouth shut. (2) He had no sympathy for his men. When he took over II Corps in the heat of North Africa, he put great emphasis on proper military dress, requiring ties, leggings and helmets at all times. He rode to the front in his Jeep painted with three yellow stars on a red background, wearing his two pearl-handled pistols. His Jeep kicked up dust or splattered mud on the battle-worn men who gave up the road to him. He was bad-tempered and thoroughly disliked by his troops. Patton lived for battles, which he believed were won by the army that hit fastest and hardest. The Germans both feared and respected his talents.

Mark CLARK had a long nose, and Churchill called him "the American Eagle." Like Patton, Clark had great energy and impatience, and was a hound for publicity. He had his own photographer, who always took pictures on his good (left) side. His ambitions caused Marshall, Eisenhower, and Bradley to be turned off by him, but Eisenhower felt that his egotistical attitude had improved, and later put him in command of the Fifth Army, formed for the invasion of Italy.

Debate

A good military leader has to have qualities that make him unique and newsworthy to succeed.

Name_____ Date _____

POINTS TO CONSIDER

1. Which top U.S. military leader would you have wanted as your commander?

_____

_____

_____

_____

_____

2. What qualities does a good military leader have?

_____

_____

_____

_____

_____

3. What qualities should a good military leader avoid?

_____

_____

_____

_____

_____

Name_____ Date _____

CHALLENGES

1. What was the characteristic that carried the most weight in Marshall's eyes?

_____

2. How did Marshall deal with Patton's problems?

_____

_____

3. What office did Marshall give Eisenhower after the United States entered the war?

_____

4. How did Eisenhower try to make the U.S. and British armies work together?

_____

_____

5. Who was "the American Bulldog," and who gave that name to him?

_____

6. What was the opinion of Bradley's men about him?

_____

_____

7. What weapon of war is associated with Patton?

_____

8. Why did Pershing say he admired Patton?

_____

_____

9. What did Patton believe won battles?

_____

10. How did Clark get the nickname "the American Eagle?"

_____

_____

THE INVASION OF SICILY AND ITALY

In 1943 Mussolini was clearly in trouble. The Italian public had seen their sons and husbands taken as prisoners of war. They had tired of Nazis coming into their towns and acting more like conquerors than allies. Members of opposition parties met secretly and plotted to overthrow Mussolini. Even Fascists worked against *Il Duce.* Many Italians had relatives in the United States and had never thought of the United States as an enemy. If American troops came, they would be seen as liberators, not occupiers.

Allied troops unloading ammunition during the invasion of Sicily

With North Africa in hand, U.S. planners expected the next target to be France, but again they bowed to British objections that such an operation was premature. The spot chosen was Sicily, the football-shaped island at the end of the boot of the Italian mainland. There were good reasons for selecting it. Attacks on Mediterranean shipping lanes would cease. Sicily could be used as the base for attacks on Greece, Yugoslavia, or southern France. Such an attack would also give training in amphibious landings under fire, which would certainly be helpful when the time to attack Italy or France came. The first step was capturing the island of Pantelleria between Sicily and Tunisia. Its 11,000-man Italian garrison put up no fight and raised the white flag. It was expected that Sicily would be a lot tougher.

A force of 180,000 Allied troops were to be transported to Sicily off the new LSTs (Landing Ship Tanks), LCTs (Landing Craft Tanks), and LCIs (Landing Craft Infantry). The LSTs carried men, and when they reached the beach, the ramp dropped, and they ran off into the water. LCTs carried the tanks and artillery needed to protect the men during the critical first few minutes of the landing. LCIs had gang planks on the side that dropped and the men went down them; they were not as seaworthy as LSTs and were adapted to other purposes after this invasion.

There were over 400,000 Axis troops on Sicily, with 90,000 Germans on the west side. Eisenhower hit the east side on July 10, 1943, with Patton's Seventh Army on the right and Montgomery's Eighth Army on the left. The Italian troops had little fight in them, but the Germans stubbornly gave ground and tried to get as many men out as possible before the island was lost. In 11 days, Sicily was in Allied hands. The competitive spirit was certainly alive, and Patton delighted in reaching Messina just ahead of Montgomery. Unfortunately, many German troops escaped.

Allied planes began flying over Italy urging the people to turn on their Axis oppressors. A conference between Mussolini and Hitler was interrupted by the report of an air raid on Rome. When Mussolini returned to the capital, he was called before the Grand Council and found that even his son-in-law was against him. The Grand Council voted 19 to 7 to give power to the king. The king forced him to resign and then had Mussolini arrested, and Marshal Pietro Badoglio took over the government. Mussolini could not believe that everyone had turned against him, even his son-in-law.

Everything seemed to be going Eisenhower's way, but trouble was just around the corner. Reports by a field hospital confirmed the story Patton had told Bradley himself. While visiting hospitals, as he often did, Patton slapped two patients suffering from shell shock with his glove, ordered them back to the front, and said that if they didn't fight, they would be shot. The press picked up the story, and it created such criticism that Eisenhower ordered Patton to apologize to the soldiers, in front of every unit in their army. Some units cheered Patton, but others stood silently. Patton was benched from then until January 1944, when he was sent to help in the preparations for D-Day.

Badoglio wanted to surrender, but Roosevelt's insistence that it must be unconditional caused problems. The Germans feared Italy might quit the war and rushed troops into northern Italy. In 1938 Hitler had vowed he would never let Mussolini go, "even if the whole world were against him." Now, true to his word, Hitler sent a rescue party into Italy to free Mussolini, and they released him on September 12, 1943.

By that time, Allied troops were on Italian soil. The invasion began September 8, with the British Eighth Army landing at Reggio on the Italian boot. That same day, British paratroops landed at Taranto. Both operations went smoothly. When U.S. and British troops landed at Salerno on the 9th, the Germans were waiting for them and gave them a hot reception. When Rangers captured the Chiunzi Pass, the beachhead was secure. Through the whole Italian campaign, the Germans were very stubborn about giving up any ground to the Allies.

The landing at Salerno was close enough that the king and government escaped to U.S. lines. The Germans marched into Rome. The Italian army simply disappeared, and its navy escaped to Malta. There was no doubt that the German army in Italy was there not as an ally, but as a ruler over a conquered land. German troops conducted raids to find workers for slave labor and to seize Jews who were taken off to concentration camps. Homes went without heat, and people were allowed only 3.5 ounces of bread per day. Mussolini was no more than a mere German puppet, hated by most of his people.

Debate

Roosevelt was wrong in demanding unconditional surrender from the Italians.

Name_____ Date _____

POINTS TO CONSIDER

1. Why didn't the Italians like the Germans anymore?

_____

_____

_____

_____

_____

2. What risks were the king and Grand Council taking in firing Mussolini?

_____

_____

_____

_____

_____

3. What were the effects of the collapse of the Italian government?

_____

_____

_____

_____

_____

Name_____ Date _____

CHALLENGES

1. How did Italians react to the possibility of an Allied invasion?

_____

_____

2. How did the Italian soldiers on Pantelleria react when the Allies came?

_____

_____

3. What different purpose did an LST have than the LCT?

_____

_____

4. Why did Eisenhower prefer hitting the east coast of Sicily?

_____

_____

5. How long did it take to conquer Sicily?

_____

6. What happened when Mussolini returned to Rome after his conference with Hitler?

_____

7. How did Patton get himself into trouble?

_____

_____

8. What did Patton have to do afterward?

_____

9. How did Hitler react to the capture of Mussolini?

_____

_____

10. How much food was allowed for Italians after the German invasion?

_____

STRUGGLING AGAINST MEN AND MOUNTAINS IN ITALY

Italy is not made for easy invasions. It is a long country, stretched out north to south, with the Apennine Mountains forming the upper spine and the Matese Mountains the east central spine. Along the northern border lie the high, beautiful, and, in wartime, deadly Alps. German Field Marshal Kesselring designed two defensive lines across central Italy: the GUSTAV LINE, which took advantage of the steep mountains and fast flowing rivers of central Italy, and in northern Italy, the GOTHIC LINE blocked the way to the Alps. No better natural line of defense existed in the European war than those mountains. The Germans were comfortable in their concrete bunkers, waiting for the Allies to reach gun range.

A stronghold on Castle Hill (center) blocked the Allied approach to Monte Cassino, the monastery at the top of the mountain.

As a bird flies, it is only about 30 miles from Salerno to Naples, but the terrain is rough. Kesselring had time to remove anything of industrial or transportation value that he could before he left Naples; the rest he destroyed. At first, the people watched as the Germans dismantled their city, but when the withdrawal began, young street fighters armed with stolen weapons attacked their oppressors. For three days the people of Naples ruled the city, until U.S. troops arrived on October 1.

Hitler accepted Kesselring's plan to draw a new line across Italy, between Naples and Rome, to be defended at all costs. To provide needed troops, two divisions were pulled from the north. Kesselring was to take charge in Italy, and Rommel was sent to protect the French coastline from a possible Allied invasion. When Eisenhower learned that more German troops were headed south, he knew Rome was not going to be easily taken.

On October 13, Marshal Badoglio announced that Italy was at war *against* Germany. That gave Italians permission to harass the German invaders, and at times, their help was needed to fight the Germans. Others were also coming in: Canadians, New Zealanders, South Africans, Gurkas from India, Poles, Free French, Algerians, and Moroccans. Even a Brazilian division arrived later. Many units had long traditions of battlefield courage to uphold.

Progress in Italy was too slow; changes were occurring that required a change in strategy. Eisenhower was leaving the Italian campaign in January 1944 to begin preparing for the Normandy invasion. Soon, many of the Allied landing craft and men were to be pulled out of Italy for use in France. So close to Rome, yet so far. A plan to land troops at Anzio, 35 miles south of Rome, had been considered and then dropped. But now, thanks to Churchill (who saw the Italian campaign as being more of a British show than American),

85

it was suddenly revived again. The attack on Anzio was scheduled for January 22. To pull Germans away from the coastline, General Fred Walker was to create a diversion by attempting to cross the Rapido River; this would pull German reserves away from the coastline. General John Lucas was to land his troops at Anzio. If they moved quickly at Anzio and reached high ground on the Alban hills, the Germans might be forced back north of Rome.

Lucas was a good officer, but he was tired and cautious. The landing went well, but instead of moving to the Alban hills, Lucas waited for more troops to arrive. When the attack across the Rapido failed, Kesselring hit the Allied troops at Anzio, and while they held their ground, they could not advance toward Rome.

In February, a new battle began, this time at Monte Cassino, a 1400-year-old monastery set on a mountaintop. The Allied commander of that sector was General Bernard Freyburg of New Zealand. It was known that the Germans had agreed not to use historic locations like this monastery for military purposes, but the Nazis had been known to lie. Freyburg wanted it bombed; Clark feared that if the bombing succeeded, the rubble would provide fine hiding places for Germans who would surely move in.

His prediction came true, and despite valiant efforts and many bombs and shells, Allied casualties were high as the men attempted to scale the mountain. Finally, on May 18, Polish troops reached the top. Their revenge on the Germans for what had happened to their country in 1939 came at a high cost, and General Clark said of them: "The Polish Corps fought with utter bravery and disregard for casualties."

The Gustav Line was broken, and on May 23 Allied troops advanced toward Rome from Anzio. Kesselring declared Rome an "open city" and began pulling back to positions farther north. Allied troops entered Rome on June 4, 1944. Two days later, the Normandy invasion began, and most attention was drawn away from the Italian campaign. After a short rest, Allied troops moved northward, one column on the east, and the other on the west; by August 11, they reached the next major barrier, the Gothic Line.

The Italian campaign was not over, but it was on hold. Allied troops in Italy became part of the invasion of southern France and were sent to help restore government to Greece after the Germans left. Many things went wrong in the Italian campaign, but it was not because of the lack of effort or courage of Allied troops.

It had served its purpose, however. It had (1) turned Italy into an ally, and the Germans felt the fury of their revenge as partisans joined Allied troops in attacking their oppressors; (2) forced the Germans to send troops there instead of to Russia or France; and (3) its unplanned effect was showing the patriotism of African-American and *Nisei* soldiers who won many medals for heroism in the Italian campaign.

Debate in 1944

Should Monte Cassino be shelled and taken, or should it be left alone, even if the Germans are using it (which is not known for certain)?

Name _____ Date _____

POINTS TO CONSIDER

1. What difference would an Italian decision to support the Allied cause make to General Clark?

_____

_____

_____

_____

_____

2. What kinds of problems would be created by sending so many nationalities into the Italian campaign? What possible benefits were there?

_____

_____

_____

_____

_____

3. Why did some soldiers in the Italian campaign later feel that their hard work was unappreciated?

_____

_____

_____

_____

_____

Name_____ Date _____

CHALLENGES

1. What two chains of mountains form the "spine" of Italy?

_____

2. What were the two German defense lines south of the Alps?

_____

3. What happened on October 13, 1943?

_____

_____

4. Who was the main person urging the landing at Anzio?

_____

5. Who led the landing at Anzio? What objective did he fail to reach?

_____

6. Who led the attack across the Rapido River? What happened to that attack?

_____

_____

7. Why did Freyburg want to bomb Monte Cassino?

_____

_____

8. Why was Clark afraid a bombing might work against the Allies?

_____

_____

9. What happened two days after Rome was captured?

_____

_____

10. What two invasions used Allied troops who had been fighting in Italy?

_____

ALLIED LEADERS DEVELOP GRAND STRATEGIES

Franklin Roosevelt and Winston Churchill were survivors of years in democratic political systems. ROOSEVELT had been a state senator, Wilson's assistant secretary of the navy, and New York's governor before being elected president in 1932. In his inaugural address, he had reassured the Depression-weary public that: "the only thing we have to fear is fear itself." During the early days of the New Deal, he was like a field general pushing the economic war on many fronts: AAA on

Seated left to right: British Prime Minister Winston Chruchill, U.S. President Franklin Roosevelt, and Soviet Prime Minister Joseph Stalin

the farm front, CCC to make jobs for young men, TVA to fight floods in the South, NRA to bring industrial recovery. In 1937 "General" Roosevelt's string of victories was ended, and some in the ranks wanted a replacement: critics like Huey Long, Father Charles Coughlin, Republicans, and Southern Democrats in Congress.

He defied the critics and American political tradition by running for a third term in 1940. Now, isolationists like the America First Committee and public figures like Charles Lindbergh opposed his efforts to help England, sure this was the path to U.S. entrance into the war.

Winston CHURCHILL graduated from Sandhurst (the British equivalent to West Point) and had served as an officer in India and the Sudan. During the Boer War he was a correspondent and, for a time, a Boer prisoner of war. After a dramatic escape, Churchill returned to England and served in Parliament from 1901 to 1916. During World War I, he commanded the Sixth Royal Fusiliers for a time, but Prime Minister Lloyd George appointed him minister of munitions. After the war, he served as secretary of state for war and colonies. In 1922 he lost his seat in Parliament, but returned in 1924; he was put in charge of finances. Defeated in 1929, he spent the next ten years writing newspaper articles warning of the need for strong antifascist policies.

When the war came, Prime Minister Chamberlain appointed him first lord of the admiralty. In 1940 when the Chamberlain government fell, Churchill was named prime minister. He told the British nation he had nothing to offer but "blood, toil, sweat and tears." He would "wage war, by sea, land and air," and his goal was summarized in one word: "Victory." His uplifted hand with the index and middle finger extended became the symbol of "V for Victory." Symbols become as important as speeches in wartime.

Roosevelt and Churchill had met briefly during World War I, and FDR admired "Winnie" greatly. They began corresponding in 1939, and a strong friendship developed. In 1940 when the British needed ships, Roosevelt sent 50 old destroyers. In March 1941 Lend-

Lease began, and U.S. naval ships began patrolling the oceans and helping the British spot subs.

In August 1941 Roosevelt and Churchill met off Newfoundland on a destroyer. Churchill (and Stalin) hoped Roosevelt was ready to declare war on Germany, but came away instead with the Atlantic Charter, which included as war aims the Four Freedoms: freedom from want and fear, and the rights to free speech and religion. Other parts picked up on themes of Wilson's Fourteen Points. A second conference was held in Washington in December 1941, and from it came the Declaration of the United Nations (January 1, 1942), which was agreed to by the 26 nations represented. It called for a united effort against the Axis, with no nation signing a separate peace. The American people enthusiastically backed it.

It was easier for FDR and Churchill to understand each other than it was for Stalin, who ran a dictatorship. The Russians were sworn enemies of capitalism, and that bothered many in Congress and Parliament. The press in the United States and Europe had rejoiced when war broke out between Germany and Russia and suggested that we let them kill each other off. Stalin felt that delays in opening a second front were for just that purpose. During the war the United States and England worked well together, but there was always some mistrust between the Western nations and Russia.

At the Casablanca Conference (January 1943), Roosevelt and Churchill met to plan the Sicily and Italy invasions and agreed there must be "unconditional surrender" before any peace treaty would be signed. Two more Roosevelt-Churchill meetings (at Washington and Quebec) were held in May and August 1943 to discuss the second front, and Secretary of State Hull went to Moscow to inform Stalin of their plan to attack France in the spring of 1944. Hull's meeting was so successful that Stalin said he would join the war against Japan after Germany was defeated.

In November 1943, the two Western leaders flew to Cairo where they met with Chiang Kai-shek. The three promised to fight until Japan surrendered unconditionally. Then, they traveled on to Teheran, Iran, to meet at last with "Uncle Joe" Stalin. The discussions (November 28–December 1) were very important. It was agreed that the second front would open in the spring of 1944, at the same time the Russians opened an offensive. There were efforts to keep discussions "light," but at times there were bitter disputes. Stalin said that 50,000 German officers should be shot after the war, an idea that outraged Churchill. Roosevelt spoke of the "Big Four" (the United States, Russia, Great Britain, and China) dominating the postwar world, but Stalin predicted that China would be weak after the war. When Stalin asked who would command the invasion, Roosevelt had to come up with an answer. After much agonizing, he told Stalin it was to be Eisenhower. Stalin was delighted.

Debate in 1944

It is good policy to require unconditional surrender before any peace treaty can be made.

90

Name_____ Date _____

POINTS TO CONSIDER

1. How do you think the political experience of Roosevelt and Churchill helped them during the war?

_____

_____

_____

_____

_____

2. If you were Stalin, would you think Lend-Lease was an act of friendship or part of a plot to kill more Russians and Germans?

_____

_____

_____

_____

_____

3. What safety measures do you think were needed for the leaders to hold meetings during wartime?

_____

_____

_____

_____

_____

Name _____ Date _____

CHALLENGES

1. How had Roosevelt approached the Depression?

_____

_____

2. What group had opposed helping England before the United States entered the war?

_____

3. On what continents had Churchill been a soldier?

_____

_____

4. What job did Churchill hold between 1929 and 1939? What was his view at that time toward the Nazis?

_____

_____

5. What one word described Churchill's goal in the war?

_____

6. What document came out of the 1941 meeting between Churchill and Roosevelt?

_____

7. What was the purpose of the Declaration of the United Nations?

_____

_____

8. Why did Stalin suspect the second front was being delayed?

_____

_____

9. What promise was made at Cairo?

_____

10. What was to happen at the same time Allied troops landed in France?

_____

PREPARING FOR D-DAY

Battles are like football games. The offense has the advantage. The coach finds weaknesses in the defense, puts players in positions where they can deceive the defenders, and takes advantage of any defense weakness. The defense has to prepare for the play based on information available and how the offensive coach has used players in the past. In war, of course, there are differences. Good defenses can not only stop the invader, but take him out of the game. Defenders already have supplies on hand and do not have to transport them under fire. They are dug in while the offense is unprotected. There are no penalties for delay of game; the attack comes when the offensive team is ready. Everyone knew in 1944 that the attack was coming, but when, where, and how, and who would lead it?

Dwight Eisenhower commanded the Allied Expeditionary Force that invaded Normandy, France.

The selection of a commander was up to Roosevelt, and even though he knew Marshall wanted it and could do it well, the president felt that Marshall was too valuable in Washington, so he selected Eisenhower.

Offense. As head of SHAEF (Supreme Headquarters, Allied Expeditionary Force), Eisenhower selected his players. Most were men he had worked with for years: Omar Bradley, Arthur Tedder, Carl Spaatz, Bedell Smith, and Bernard Montgomery. One big question was the role Charles de Gaulle should play; Eisenhower decided he should be involved because of his ties to French resistance. Eisenhower began working on the game plan.

Defense. Leading the defense was General Rundstedt (commander in chief, west). Preparation to build an "Atlantic Wall" began in 1942, but Rundstedt reported in October 1943 that defenses were inadequate and more troops were needed. Hitler began beefing up his line and sent Rommel to France to command coastal defenses. Rommel's authority was limited to a line 15–20 miles along the coast. The *Panzers*, navy, and *Luftwaffe* were not under his command. Rommel wanted land mines and beach obstacles, Rundstedt wanted tanks to provide firepower where it was needed. Rommel protested that tanks would be destroyed by Allied planes before they got into the battle. The Panzer commander, General Schweppenburg, appealed to General Jodl of the High Command for permission to keep his tanks at a safe distance from Allied naval artillery. The request was granted.

Offense. Eisenhower was having trouble controlling his situation as well. Patton created trouble with a speech he gave; Marshall and Eisenhower were fed up with Patton and came close to sending him home. The person in charge of the U.S. Strategic Air Force (bombers) was Carl Spaatz. He had to be convinced that his planes should strike transportation lines. Spaatz wanted to hit aircraft plants and oil refineries (bigger targets were easier to hit in night bombing raids). After much debate, Eisenhower finally gave the order to hit transportation.

Deceptions. It was important that the Germans be misled as to where the landing would take place. Operation Fortitude was a plan to make the Germans believe that the allies would strike at Calais and not Normandy. Operation Fortitude North made the Germans believe the landing site was Norway. The British created a nonexistent Fourth Army of 350,000 men in Scotland to attack. Operation Fortitude South made the Germans believe Belgium and northern France were the targets. Operation Glimmer was to make them expect the attack at Bologne. A notable failure was Operation Copperhead (or Hambone), which involved sending an actor, who looked almost exactly like Montgomery, to Gibraltar. On the way, he got drunk and came off the plane smoking a cigar (Monty did not smoke or drink). He was sent back.

Of these deceptions, the most effective was Fortitude. Its leader was General Patton, the man the Germans thought was the most likely leader. They believed the whole slapping incident and the criticism of Patton for speeches he had given was an effort to mislead them. Patton's army was equipped with inflated rubber tanks, fake radio communications, and phony hospitals, ammunition dumps, camps, guns, and planes all made of canvas.

Build-up. Deception was only a small part of the game; the build-up of men, equipment, food, medical supplies, LSTs (Landing Ship Tanks), ships, planes, gliders, parachutes, oil, and gasoline required much detailed planning. So much equipment and so many supplies came that it was said the barrage balloons were there to keep the island afloat. Intelligence gathering was very important. French Resistance spies stole blueprints for bunkers and overheard conversations. Planes flew over France taking detailed pictures.

While the men went through their "dress rehearsals," storming English beaches, scaling cliffs, and loading supplies on LSTs, ships, and planes, Eisenhower attended last minute briefings, visited as many units as possible, and watched the sky. Weather was the one thing that could not be planned. SHAEF's chief meteorologist was British Captain J.M. Stagg. He predicted stormy weather on June 5 but an improvement from that afternoon until the evening of June 6. Whether to go or not was Eisenhower's decision alone. After considering the risks, he smiled and said: "OK, we'll go." Rommel's meteorologist predicted bad weather continuing through June 6, and he went home to visit his family.

By June 6, 1944, Rundstedt had 58 divisions. It would take two weeks for the Allies to have as many men in France as the Germans, when it was best to outnumber defenders 3–1. Coach Eisenhower knew exactly what he was up against. The time had come. The offensive team was ready.

Debate in May 1944

What are the best targets for bombing runs: transportation lines or refineries?

Name_____ Date _____

POINTS TO CONSIDER

1. If you had commanded the operation, how would you have kept the real destination secret?

_____

_____

_____

_____

_____

2. If you were in charge of food distribution, what problems would you have?

_____

_____

_____

_____

_____

3. What worries did Eisenhower have on the evening of June 5, 1944?

_____

_____

_____

_____

_____

Name _____ Date _____

CHALLENGES

1. In battles, which side has the advantage in supplies?

_____

2. Which side has the advantage in timing?

_____

3. Why was De Gaulle involved?

_____

_____

4. What was Rommel's role in the Atlantic Wall?

_____

_____

5. Why did Schweppenburg want his tanks back from the shore?

_____

_____

6. What targets did Eisenhower want bombers to hit, and what targets did Spaatz prefer? Underline the targets that were chosen.

_____

7. What was the purpose of Operation Fortitude North?

_____

_____

8. Who "commanded" Operation Fortitude?

_____

9. What was J.M. Stagg's job?

_____

_____

10. Who said "OK, we'll go"?

_____

D-DAY ARRIVES

June 5, 1944, was a stormy, sleep-less night for those on the coast of Normandy, France, whether in the LSTs offshore, the bombers and gliders over-head, the concrete bunkers on the beach, or among the partisans moving into posi-tion to disrupt German troop movements to the beach. Night air raids had become common, but this one seemed worse hour by the hour. On board the LSTs and transports, chaplains prayed, and the crowded men were deep in thoughts of family, home, and fear that they might not measure up.

The Nazi defenders were not sure what was going on. Their radar stations had been bombed, the *Luftwaffe* had been grounded, and the naval ships re-mained in the harbor because of the

The successful assault on the beaches of Normandy, France, allowed Allied troops to break the German's Atlantic Wall and start pushing them back towards Germany.

storm. Railroads had been battered and telephone lines cut. The weather had been so bad that many defenders relaxed, thinking that no attack would come in such miserable weather. Many German division commanders were away from their units attending a war game where the subject was a naval assault on Normandy.

At Calais, the few remaining German radars began picking up signals produced by clever British engineers. Echoes of troop transports were made by reflector balloons carried by motor launches, and strips of aluminum foil dropped from RAF bombers simulated more planes. Most Luftwaffe planes in the region were rushed to Calais to stop the invaders.

The beaches of Normandy had been given code names by the planners: from left to right, the beaches were named Utah, Omaha, Gold, Juno, and Sword. Utah and Omaha were to be taken by U.S. troops, the others by British and Canadian troops. U.S. parachute and glider drops behind enemy lines at Utah were to precede the landing; British drops were behind the lines at Sword beach.

The first British paratroopers and gliders landed shortly after midnight, and using clickers to find each other in the darkness, formed units and began completing their assignments. The most difficult job went to a British paratroop battalion that was to take out guns surrounded by a barbed wire tangle, an antitank ditch, and machine gun nests. The guns were in a blockhouse with steel doors and thick concrete walls. Despite the obstacles, they succeeded, and saved many lives as a result.

A slow German reaction time was critical to success. At 1:11 A.M., a phone call awakened a general informing him of the parachute drops. Word reached Rommel's chief of staff at about 2:15, but he did not believe this was the real invasion. However, he sent the message on to Runstedt. At 2:55, he sent the message to Berlin, but he was still not sure whether the attack was at Normandy or Calais. By 4:15 Runstedt concluded that Normandy was the invasion site and ordered available reserves to Normandy. He sent a message to

Jodl asking for approval. Jodl was not awakened until 6:30; he angrily denied the order for reserves since it had been done without permission. At that same time, observers looked out at the ocean and saw hundreds of ships and LSTs on the horizon. Then the naval barrage began, and the ground shook along the 50-mile invasion front.

The landing was a huge operation: 150,000 men, 12,000 planes, 1,500 tanks, 5,300 ships. They were equipped with new machines never used before in war: portable harbors called Mullberries, flail tanks with big chains on them to pound the ground and explode mines (Crabs), amphibious tanks called DDs, and Crocodile tanks that shot flame instead of shells.

Brigadier General Theodore Roosevelt, Jr., a veteran of three other landings, went with the men landing at Utah Beach. Fortunately for them, they were 2,000 yards away from the assigned landing site. Their beach was deserted, and they moved quickly inland. Omaha Beach was much more dangerous and losses there were heavy. Defensive positions were on cliffs that were hard to reach. Brigadier General Norman Cotta arrived on Omaha Beach at 7:30 and found that the men were terrified. Finding some Rangers, he said: "If you're Rangers, get up and lead the way." They took the challenge and climbed the cliff. The Canadians and British struggled at their beaches, but once past them, began to move inland. In one day, the Atlantic Wall was cracked.

It was fortunate for the Allies that D-Day was a success, because a week later, on June 12, the Germans launched their first V–1 rockets on England. Nicknamed "buzz bombs" and "doodle bugs," they flew at a maximum speed of 150 to 250 miles per hour (mph) and at an altitude of 2,000 to 3,000 feet. Cheap to build, they were designed for bombing large urban areas since they had no guidance systems. V-1s dropped with a high-pitched sound warning of their arrival. V–1s were so slow that many were shot down by the RAF or antiaircraft fire.

V–2s were much more sophisticated. First used in September 1944, they flew at up to an altitude of 120 miles, then dropped at 2,000 mph. No defense could stop them. They often made a crater 30 feet deep when they crashed, so much of their explosion was muffled by the ground.

German technology also produced the ME–262, a jet aircraft capable of flying 540 mph, much faster than any Allied plane. It came out in April 1944, and Luftwaffe pilots saw this as a tremendous interceptor. Hitler demanded that its wings be strengthened to make it a bomber. When it did intercept Allied bombers, it flew so fast it had to be slowed down to hit its target. Of the 220 used in combat, 120 were shot down.

If the invasion had been delayed or defeated, these attacks would have changed the war and given Germany time to develop other weapons.

Debate

Success at Normandy came more from good planning than from luck and enemy mistakes.

Name _____ Date _____

POINTS TO CONSIDER

1. Cooped up on an LST waiting to hit the beach, what would you have been thinking about?

_____

_____

_____

_____

_____

2. How much depended on successful use of science and technology?

_____

_____

_____

_____

3. Why were V–1s and V–2s more of a threat than the Luftwaffe to cities like London?

_____

_____

_____

_____

Name _____ Date _____

CHALLENGES

1. What had the Allies done to interrupt German defense of Normandy?

_____

_____

2. What was the effect of the storm?

_____

_____

3. What simple devices made the Germans believe the landing was going to be at Calais?

_____

_____

4. What city and state were honored by having Normandy landing beaches named after them?

_____

5. How long was it between the time of the first phone call to a general until Jodl was contacted?

_____

6. Why did Jodl reject the sending of troops to Normandy?

_____

_____

7. How long was the invasion area?

_____

8. How many men and ships were involved?

_____

9. What were two nicknames given V–1s?

_____

10. What was the fastest airplane used in the war?

_____

EFFORTS TO END THE HITLER ERA

A big disadvantage for dictators is that any who dislike them or their policies have no way to express that opinion openly and must resort to plots against their ruler. From the beginning, Nazi opponents were punished, but a few continued to protest publicly, and others even acted.

In occupied areas, Nazis did what conquerors have always done. They wanted the people to know who the masters were. An individual could do little by himself or herself, and it was hard to know whom to trust. Once reliable anti-Nazis formed themselves as the Resistance movement, they needed training if they were to be used in sabotage or espionage. Helpful information was provided by SOE (Special Operations Executive) in London. Supplies and equipment came by submarines or air drops. Coded messages were included in regular BBC (British Broadcasting Corporation) radio broadcasts. At first the

Hitler survived all assassination attempts and got rid of those who opposed his authority.

conquered people showed little interest. The U.S. Declaration of Independence had noted the reason in 1776: "Mankind are more disposed to suffer, while evils are sufferable, than to right themselves by abolishing the forms to which they are accustomed."

When the occupied people were finally fed up with citizens being sent to work for the Third Reich, being treated like animals, national art treasures being sent to Göering's private collection, and food rations cut for civilians while Nazi officers ate more, the Resistance grew. In every case of sabotage, the Germans rounded up townspeople with no pretext of discovering who was guilty and then shot them in a public execution.

Outside Germany, resistance was patriotic, but German protesters could be accused of treason. Some who defied Hitler and public opinion were ministers and priests opposing the Nazis' twisted version of Christianity. In Nazi religion, the Old Testament was not suitable for Germans, Christ was a Nordic killed by Jews, and Hitler was the new Messiah.

Among Protestant ministers arrested were Dr. Karl Barth (fired from the University of Bonn for refusing to give the Nazi salute or start sermons with "Heil Hitler"), Dr. Dietrich Bonhöffer (executed at a concentration camp), and Dr. Martin Niemöller (sent to a concentration camp but saved from execution by his World War I record as a submarine commander). Catholics had trouble with the Nazis as well. In 1937 Pope Pius XI ordered that a statement be read in every church that charged Hitler with exposing Catholics to illegal and inhuman violence. Two bishops angering the Nazis were Cardinal Galen of Münster, whose protests stopped the execution of the mentally ill in 1941, and Bishop Faulhaber, who helped Munich's Chief Rabbi save religious objects during the *Kristallnacht* riots.

A few brave individuals protested, but certain army officers were the ones who acted. General Werner Von Fritsch was shocked by Nazi violations of civil rights. False charges were brought against him, but he was found not guilty by a military court and returned to the army. Fritsch wrote of Hitler: "If he goes down, he will drag us all down with him—there is nothing we can do." During the Battle of Poland, he exposed himself to enemy fire and was killed. General Ludwig Beck resigned as chief of the army general staff to protest the proposed Czech invasion in 1938. He began looking for officers willing to help overthrow Hitler. Early plots to arrest Hitler failed, but the brutality of the SS and battlefield defeats increased the numbers of officers desperate for a change in leadership.

The assassination plot of July 21, 1944, was code named Operation Valkyrie and was to be carried out by Colonel Claus von Stauffenberg who had lost one eye, part of an arm, and had only three fingers on the other one. His chance came when Hitler met with him and other officers at Rastenburg. The colonel carried bombs in brief cases, which he placed under the heavy oak table in the room. With explosives set to go off in five minutes, Stauffenberg left the room. The explosion caved the roof in, and he heard the sounds of the injured screaming and groaning. He got through checkpoints to his plane and flew away not knowing whether Hitler was dead or alive.

Stauffenberg and Beck met in Berlin and planned to take over the government. They contacted other conspirators by phone, and some began to act. Then the message came on Berlin radio that the führer had survived and would speak that evening. When they were arrested by the SS, Beck was allowed to shoot himself. Stauffenberg and many others were executed. Before it was over, 7,000 were found guilty of either being involved or sympathetic to the guilty.

A serious problem the Nazis had was how to deal with the very popular Rommel. He was not involved in the plot, but only because he had been wounded by a low-flying British fighter plane. Rommel was allowed to take a quick-acting poison, and after he died, it was reported that he died from his wounds. He was given a big funeral, and expressions of grief came from Hitler and other high government officials. Stauffenberg's family was not as fortunate as Rommel's. Anyone with the name, whether related directly to the colonel or not, was arrested. Some went to prison, and their children were sent to concentration camps.

Hitler had survived the failed plot, but indirectly it shortened the war by depriving the führer of some of his best military officers.

Debate

Killing Hitler was the moral thing to do.

Name _____ Date _____

POINTS TO CONSIDER

1. What do you think were the reactions of townspeople to the executions?

_____

_____

_____

_____

_____

2. How did Nazi religion differ from Catholic and Protestant teachings?

_____

_____

_____

_____

_____

3. If after each incident of sabotage more innocent people were executed, why did the resistance movement continue to grow?

_____

_____

_____

_____

_____

CHALLENGES

1. Why did the Nazis create dislike for themselves in occupied areas?

_____

_____

2. What group supplied sabotage and espionage equipment to the Resistance?

_____

3. What was a common method of delivering messages to the Resistance?

_____

_____

4. Which Protestant minister's World War I record saved him from execution?

_____

5. What did Pope Pius XI accuse the Nazis of doing?

_____

6. Which church official spoke out against the execution of the mentally ill?

_____

7. How did the Nazis try to get rid of General Fritsch?

_____

_____

8. Who began the plotting against Hitler?

_____

9. Why did Stauffenberg feel confident that he had succeeded?

_____

_____

10. How many were found guilty of being involved or sympathetic to the attempt?

_____

CONCENTRATION CAMPS: CENTERS FOR GENOCIDE

Even in its beginning, the Nazi regime was cruel. Captured resistance workers, conquered Polish and Russian civilians, and Russian prisoners of war were victims of oppression. At best their needs were neglected; at worst they were tortured, deliberately starved, or worked to death. The SS found special pleasure in dealing with the "subhuman" Jews, gypsies, insane, and deformed. Reinhard Heydrich, the "Blond Beast," was the head of the SD, which specialized in carrying out Hitler's Jewish policies.

The concentration camps were centers for carrying out Hitler's policy of exterminating the Jews.

Two terms are important in understanding Hitler's "Final Solution" for the Jewish problem. *Holocaust* is defined as "a great or complete devastation or destruction." *Genocide* is "deliberate extermination of a national, racial, political, or cultural group." Hitler wanted Europe's Jewish population entirely destroyed.

In September 1941 Hitler ordered that all German Jews be shipped to the ghettos (Jewish sections) of Polish cities. That December the camp at Chelmno opened to "clear" Jews from the annexed area. They were killed as soon as they arrived.

In 1942 two British-trained Czechs killed Heydrich near Prague. In revenge Hitler put his finger on a map and picked the town of Lidice to be destroyed. The men were murdered, the women sent to concentration camps, and the children sent to Germany to be raised as Nazis. Heydrich's replacement was Ernst Kaltenbrunner, a huge brute of a man who devoted his energies to finding new ways to kill.

Some of the most cruel people in human history worked in the concentration camps. A few became notorious. Adolf Eichmann was the SD Jewish expert. Even though he claimed that he had nothing personal against the Jews, he sent millions to their deaths. His motto was "obey," but Eichmann continued gassing Jews even after Himmler ordered him to stop in 1944. Dr. Josef Mengele was the "angel of death." A man with the "face of an angel," he met trains coming into Auschwitz. As people got off the cattle cars, he decided with his thumb to the right or left who was to be gassed and who lived a little longer. Mengele was responsible for the deaths of 400,000 Jews.

Some of the larger prison camps will be remembered for centuries to come. DACHAU was the first concentration camp (1933), and its gate mocked the new inmates with the words *"Arbeit Macht Frei"* (Work Brings Freedom). BUCHENWALD was located near Weimar and was used to provide labor for local arms factories. Deaths averaged 6,000 a month, but survival chances were better there than in other camps.

The large extermination camps were in Poland. The three largest were Auschwitz, Maidanek, and Treblinka. AUSCHWITZ was the largest; at its peak, it housed 100,000 prisoners with 12,000 killed per day. Its gas chambers could execute 2,000 at a time using

Zyclon B gas. The prisoners were told they were going to shower and to remove all of their clothes. Once packed inside, gas poured from the shower heads, and death followed 3 to 15 minutes later. TREBLINKA received 5,000 Jews a day from the Warsaw ghetto; all were sent to "shower" after they arrived. In two months in 1942, 300,000 died there. MAIDANEK had some work projects, but it was mainly a mass murder factory; about 1.5 million were gassed there.

The dead were robbed of anything of value, including their hair, gold teeth, watches, and jewelry. The hair was used for lining army boots. Gold paid for the expense of the war machine; watches and jewelry were given to the SS and wounded soldiers. Clothes were given to the poor. Stealing any of this wealth was a death penalty offense, but some camp officials built large bank accounts. Another way that money could be made was by renting prisoners out. In return for a small payment, Jewish laborers were rented out to private companies. If they died from overwork or starvation, it was no problem. Bribes were given to the officials providing the laborers, increasing corruption in the concentration camp management system.

The years of suffering and malnutrition weakened the prisoners' desire for revolt or revenge, but occasionally, they struck back. By January 1943 the once crowded Warsaw ghetto had only 60,000 remaining Jews, and the Nazis intended to eliminate them. Armed with smuggled guns, the Jews forced the Germans to retreat. More arms came in from the outside, and the defenders fought to the last man. The battle ended in April.

Treblinka inmates stole grenades and rifles from the arsenal and surprised the guards with a sudden attack. About 150 to 200 got away, but they were easily picked off one by one, and very few survived the war.

What is remarkable about the Holocaust is not that six million Jews died, but that many survived. Christians risked their own lives by hiding Jews or helping them escape. Danes saved 90 percent of their Jews, the French 78 percent, but the Dutch could only save 25 percent of theirs.

Only Holocaust survivors know how truly bad conditions were in these camps. Allied soldiers who liberated the camps were shocked by the conditions. When Eisenhower and Patton visited the camp at Ohrdruf, it was even worse than they had imagined it, and Patton became so ill that he vomited. Eisenhower ordered every soldier not at the front lines to come to the camp, so that if they did not understand what they were fighting for, at least they would know what they were fighting against.

Debate

Guards at concentration camps who only followed orders and were not involved in the torture of prisoners were war criminals.

Name_____ Date _____

POINTS TO CONSIDER

1. Do you think the Nazis who ran concentration camps were just obeying orders as they claimed?

_____

_____

_____

_____

_____

2. How could a greedy camp commander make a profit from his job?

_____

_____

_____

_____

_____

3. Why might a Christian help Jews he barely knew to escape the camps?

_____

_____

_____

_____

_____

Name _____ Date _____

CHALLENGES

1. What is a holocaust?

_____

_____

2. What is the purpose of genocide?

_____

_____

3. Where were German Jews shipped in 1941?

_____

4. For what crime did the innocent people of Lidice suffer?

_____

_____

5. What doctor was known as the "angel of death"?

_____

6. What did the sign on Dachau's gate mean in English?

_____

7. How many inmates were killed at Auschwitz each day?

_____

8. How many Jews were killed at Maidanek?

_____

9. What happened to the watches and jewelry of those executed?

_____

_____

10. What percentage of Denmark's Jewish population survived the war?

_____

THE U.S. NAVY'S TURKEY SHOOT

The Japanese navy suffered heavy losses during the Battle of the Philippine Sea. The carriers *Shokaku* and *Hiyo* were both sunk.

Allied victory in the war depended on land, air, and sea power. The effectiveness of the naval bombardment of German coastal guns at Normandy was important to the landing's success. Pacific campaigns in New Guinea and the Solomon, Marshall, and Mariana Islands demonstrated that without a strong navy, successful land operations were impossible.

This article will deal with some of the ships and boats used by the United States against Japan and will then focus on the Battle of the Philippine Sea.

AIRCRAFT CARRIERS. The United States, Great Britain, and Japan were the three great aircraft carrier nations during the war. Carriers were especially important in the Pacific, and in battles like the Coral Sea and Midway, they were critical to success. U.S. carriers were named after famous battles or historic U.S. Navy ships: *Ticonderoga, Lexington, Yorktown, Essex, Enterprise,* and so on. The quality of U.S. carriers improved during the war, and the planes they carried also improved, with such planes as the F6F Hellcat and the F4U Corsair flying off their decks by the end of the war.

BATTLESHIPS. The U.S. Navy had 15 battleships in 1939, and 15 others were built during the war. With their large 14- to 16-inch guns (shells of a 16-inch gun are 16 inches in diameter) they could fire shells weighing a ton up to 25 miles. Because battleships were large, they also made easy targets. Japan had 12 at the beginning of the war and added the giant *Yamato* and *Musashi* in 1941 and 1942; none survived the war. U.S. battleships were named for states.

CRUISERS. Smaller and faster than battleships, U.S. cruisers usually had six- or eight-inch guns. They were involved in many troop landings and naval battles. U.S. cruisers were named for cities.

DESTROYERS. Armed with five-inch guns, destroyers were the most numerous class of U.S. ship in the war. They acted as escorts to larger ships, helped to end the submarine menace, and sometimes fought battleships. U.S. destroyers were named for navy men.

MINESWEEPERS had the job of exploding mines that had been set by the enemy in shipping lanes. Some mines were on the surface (floaters), but others were below the surface. Low-flying aircraft could spot them in clear water as deep as five fathoms.

MOTOR TORPEDO BOATS (They were called PTs by Americans, MTBs by the British) were used effectively against enemy merchant and naval ships. U.S. boats were designated by number, the most famous being John F. Kennedy's PT–109.

SUBMARINES. The Germans and Japanese both had large submarine fleets at the beginning of the war, but they did not improve them during the war and many were sunk. British subs were used mostly in the Mediterranean. The U.S. Navy started the war with old subs and torpedoes that misfired, but by the end of the war, it had the best sub fleet at sea. During the war, subs sank 1,000 Japanese merchant ships and about one-third of all Japanese warships that went down. The leader in kills was the *Tautog* with 26 followed by the *Tang* with 24. They had many other jobs as well: scouting for aircraft carriers, laying mines, rescuing fliers, and so on. U.S. subs were named for fish.

Besides weapons, U.S. ships had two big advantages: radar to pick up approaching ships and aircraft, and knowledge of the Japanese code.

The Battle of the Philippine Sea (June 19–20, 1944) off the Mariana Islands was one of those battles that had an important influence on the outcome of the Pacific war. It involved many types of surface ships and subs. Of the two fleets in the Philippine Sea, the United States outnumbered the Japanese 15–9 in carriers, 7–5 in battleships, 21–13 in cruisers, and 69–28 in destroyers. In total aircraft engaged, the United States outnumbered the Japanese 956–473, but the Japanese aircraft had longer ranges than the American planes.

The Japanese, under Admiral Ozawa, put much of their fleet into this battle. The U.S. fleet was under the command of Admiral Raymond Spruance, and leading the carrier-based aircraft was Admiral Marc Mitscher. Spruance had orders to protect Saipan, so rather than move out to attack the Imperial Japanese Navy (IJN), he waited for them to come to him. His first line of defense was an air screen; the second was a line of destroyers and cruisers. Behind them were the four carriers. Battleships protected Saipan.

The sub *Cavalla* spotted the Japanese task force approaching and sent word to Mitscher. Another sub, the *Albacore,* spotted the *IJN Taiho,* a very large aircraft carrier, and hit the *Taiho* with three of its torpedoes. Later in the day, the *Cavalla* sank the carrier *Shokaku.* As if that was not enough disaster for the Japanese, the air war was even worse. Warned by radar of enemy planes approaching, Hellcats went up to meet them. Of 69 Japanese planes in the first wave, only 11 reached U.S. destroyers, and their only hit was one bomb on the *South Dakota.* A pilot compared it to a turkey shoot back home, and the battle became known as the "Great Marianas Turkey Shoot."

The second day of battle was even more lopsided. On June 20, U.S. planes attacked as the sun was going down and sank the carrier *Hiyo* and three tankers. They also badly damaged two other carriers, a battleship, and a heavy cruiser. The attack that day cost the United States only 18 planes.

When the battle began, the IJN had 430 planes on its carriers; as the fleet retreated, it had only 35 left. The battle cost the United States 80 planes and 50 pilots. After that battle, Japanese troops on the Pacific islands could count on little naval or air support, and the navy could not replace the ships, planes, and crews that had been lost.

Debate

In light of the Battle of the Philippine Sea and other battles, did the U.S. Navy deserve more credit than the army or marines?

Name _____ Date _____

POINTS TO CONSIDER

1. If you were going to build a navy and could only use two classes of ships or boats, which would you choose? Why?

_____

_____

_____

_____

_____

2. What benefits did radar and knowledge of the enemy code give?

_____

_____

_____

_____

_____

3. Why do you think that Admiral Ozawa wanted to fight this battle even though the odds were against him?

_____

_____

_____

_____

_____

Name_____ Date _____

CHALLENGES

1. What type of a ship was the *U.S.S. Indianapolis?*

_____

2. What type of a ship was the *U.S.S. Missouri?*

_____

3. What type of a ship was the *U.S.S. Saratoga?*

_____

4. What type of a boat was the *U.S.S. Starfish?*

_____

5. What were two carrier-based aircraft that were used by the United States?

_____

_____

6. What was a "floater"?

_____

_____

7. Which sub had the highest number of kills, and how many ships did it sink?

_____

_____

8. How many total ships were involved in the Battle of the Philippine Sea for the United States? For Japan?

_____

_____

9. How many IJN carriers were sunk or badly damaged in the battle?

_____

10. How many carrier-based planes did the Japanese lose in the battle?

_____

_____

LIBERATING THE PHILIPPINES

Many unkind things were said about the Japanese during the war, but those who fought them never described them as "cowards." By 1943 the Japanese were losing ships, planes, and men that they could no longer replace. Among those casualties was their great Admiral Yamamoto. He was a casualty of U.S. code breaking; code breakers learned that he was flying to Bougainville and ambushed him as he landed. U.S. power was growing as new ships joined the fleet. Yet, as Allied forces moved ever closer, Japanese determination seemed to grow stronger. After the Battle of the

Genral Douglas MacArthur returned to the Philippines in October 1944.

Philippine Sea, the islands of Saipan, Guam, and Tinian fell to advancing U.S. forces, but three major island battles and a final naval battle were yet to be fought.

MacArthur's departure from the Philippines had been less than glorious. Escaping on a PT boat, he reached Australia, where he vowed: "I shall return." He was anxious to fulfill that promise. The island selected for that landing was Leyte; it had a good harbor, wide beaches, and six airports that could be used for future expansion in the islands.

On October 12, 1944, young Japanese pilots hit Halsey's fleet returning from attacks on Luzon, Okinawa, and Formosa. They eagerly reported a marvelous victory; their attack had sunk 19 carriers and several battleships, cruisers, and destroyers. Actually, only two cruisers had been damaged. As Admiral Halsey expected, this "victory" would draw the Japanese fleet out to finish off the crippled Americans. Japanese Admiral Shima sent cruisers and destroyers out for that purpose, but when they saw the U.S. fleet still intact, they wisely withdrew. Halsey informed Nimitz by radio: "All third fleet ships recently reported sunk by radio Tokyo have been salvaged and are retiring at high speed toward the Japanese fleet." The Japanese navy did not inform the army of their mistake, and the army sent more men from Luzon to Leyte.

The attack on Leyte began with a two-day naval shelling followed by an amphibious landing on October 20. When the beach was secure, MacArthur and his staff made a dramatic arrival, splashing through the waters of the beach. Taking a microphone, he broadcast a radio message to the Filipinos and the world: "I have returned! By the grace of Almighty God, our forces stand again on Philippine soil." He asked civilians to help win the victory. Three days later, President Sergio Osmena and MacArthur announced that civil government had been restored to the Philippines.

The Japanese had different ideas. Admiral Toyoda planned to lure Halsey out to attack his four aircraft carriers, and while they were on a "fishing expedition," his nine battleships would destroy the smaller ships left behind to supply and protect Leyte. On October 22, 1944, two U.S. subs sighted 5 battleships, 12 cruisers, and 10–12 destroyers of one fleet

113

heading toward Leyte. Their torpedoes sank two cruisers and crippled another. In the surface battle that followed, the Japanese lost a large battleship.

This was the first of four naval engagements called the Battle of Leyte Gulf, which continued from October 23 to 26, 1944. It was the largest naval battle in history because of the number of ships involved and the expanse of area it covered.

Admiral Onishi came up with a new approach to combat, the *kamikazes*. These were young fliers who volunteered for suicide missions. The planes they flew were old, and each carried a 550-pound bomb. The plan of attack was simple: aim the plane at a ship and die for the emperor. There were more volunteers than there were planes, and after a man was chosen, he might be called in a few days or wait months to go on his last mission.

The total losses in the Battle of Leyte Gulf for Japan were 3 large carriers, 4 smaller carriers, 4 battleships, 14 cruisers, 32 destroyers, and 11 subs. U.S. losses were 4 small carriers, 6 destroyers, 3 destroyer escorts, and 7 subs. The Japanese were no longer a threat to the Philippine invasion.

After Leyte was in hand, MacArthur wanted to take Luzon. The largest island of the Philippines, it was also home to the capital city of Manila. He planned to attack the south side of the island, draw the Japanese down, and then land in the north and have them trapped between his armies. The attack on Luzon had to wait until the navy had repaired and resupplied its ships. It was finally conducted in January 1945. Some of the U.S. forces met only light opposition, because General Yamashita had pulled his troops back into mountain strongholds. The Japanese air force used all 200 planes available, with kamikazes causing extensive damage on some U.S. ships.

The IJN began defending Manila from the U.S. forces coming into the city in February 1945. They destroyed the city's power plant and looted and burned Filipino homes and shops. During the Japanese occupation, Filipinos remained very loyal to the United States and were punished severely for it. A bitter street-to-street struggle lasted until March 3. By that time little of the city remained intact. As tanks broke through the concrete walls around Santo Tomas University, they found 4,000 ill-clad, starving people inside. The survivors of the Bataan Death March had finally been found, with bones clearly visible and skulls too large for their frames. As they stood at attention, they showed that pride had not been lost.

In the mountains, fighting continued until September 2, 1945, when General Yamashita surrendered. His ragged army had suffered from hunger, a shortage of ammunition, and attacks by Filipino guerrillas.

MacArthur had kept his promise to return, and in 1946 the United States kept its promise to grant independence to the Philippines.

Debate

Were kamikaze pilots brave or were they foolish?

Name _____ Date _____

POINTS TO CONSIDER

1. If you were planning a landing on an island, what factors would you need to keep in mind?

_____

_____

_____

_____

_____

2. What did Halsey mean in the statement that was quoted?

_____

_____

_____

_____

3. Why did young men volunteer to be kamikaze pilots?

_____

_____

_____

_____

Name _____ Date _____

CHALLENGES

1. Where was Yamamoto killed?

_____

2. How many carriers did Japanese pilots think they sank on October 12? How many were actually sunk?

_____

_____

3. What statement had MacArthur made after he left the Philippines?

_____

4. Why did Shima's fleet pull back?

_____

_____

5. Who were kamikaze pilots?

_____

_____

6. How many missions did a kamikaze pilot fly to fulfill his duty?

_____

7. How many battleships and cruisers (total) did Japan lose in the Leyte Gulf, and how many did the United States lose?

_____

_____

8. On what island is Manila located?

_____

9. Why was opposition to U.S. troops so light much of the time?

_____

_____

10. When did General Yamashita surrender?

_____

THE UNUSUAL POLITICS OF WARTIME ELECTIONS

The U.S. Constitution requires that the presidential election be held every four years, and it is to the credit of the nation that not even the Civil War in 1864 or World War II in 1944 were used by the president as an excuse to cancel or postpone it. Still, wartime elections are unique. It is hard for the opposition party to attack the president's policies when it gives aid and comfort to an enemy. The usual topics of taxes and domestic programs are less on the public mind than progress of the war.

There are certain truths in U.S. politics. (1) The party out of power often gains in off-year elections when there is

Although Franklin Roosevelt had many critics, he was re-elected for a fourth term in 1944.

no presidential contest. (2) Economic matters are important, but so is the way the public views other national events (like wars). (3) The popularity of the president depends on a wide variety of issues, and no one can predict at the beginning of a campaign which issues will be important to voters at the end of it.

Franklin Roosevelt (FDR) had been president since 1933. During his time in office he had offended conservatives who feared that he was leading the nation to socialism, business leaders who felt that he was too pro-labor, taxpayers critical of waste in New Deal programs, and those who felt that he had been in office too long. If two terms were enough for Washington and Jefferson, why did Roosevelt need four? Besides, the Depression and war years had aged the president, and many questioned whether he could last until 1948. The Democrats warned against changing horses in the middle of the stream; Republicans said that with Roosevelt, we were always in the middle of the stream.

In 1942 the war was going badly: the Dutch East Indies, Bataan, Corregidor, Wake Island, Guam, and even two islands of the Alaska chain fell to Japan. The war against the European fascists wasn't going much better: Nazis were at the gates of Moscow and moving toward the Suez Canal. The attack on North Africa was scheduled for November 8, five days after the off-year election. On the other hand, the economy was growing rapidly, and unemployment was no longer at crisis figures. In 1940, 14.6 percent were unemployed; in 1942, only 4.7 percent did not have jobs. The 1940 elections had given the Democrats a lead over House Republicans of 268–162. But in 1942 that lead was cut to 218–208, and the Senate makeup of 66–28 dropped to 58–37. Southern Democrats were as opposed to some New Deal programs as Republicans; clearly Roosevelt's strength had been weakened.

As the 1944 election approached, there were good signs for the Democrats. Unemployment was down to only 1.2 percent, factories were running two or three shifts, and the war was going well in both Europe and Asia. But they had problems as well. (1) Vice President

Henry Wallace was very unpopular. (2) Roosevelt was showing his age; he looked tired and did not speak with his old dynamic force. (3) The public was getting tired of wartime restrictions. (4) Critics said that Roosevelt was going too far in asking for a fourth term. (5) The general feeling was that Democrats were antibusiness, but postwar prosperity depended on business growth.

The Republicans passed over Wendell Willkie and Douglas MacArthur and chose Governor Thomas E. Dewey of New York as their presidential candidate, with Governor John Bricker of Ohio as his running mate. At the insistence of some of his political advisors, Roosevelt dumped Wallace from the ticket and chose Senator Harry Truman for a running mate. Truman was best known at the time for the Truman Committee that had uncovered many cases of overcharging by defense contractors and saved billions of dollars for the government.

Dewey charged: "This is a campaign against an Administration which was conceived in defeatism, which failed for eight straight years to restore our domestic economy, which has been the most wasteful, extravagant and incompetent Administration in the history of the nation."

As often happens in political campaigns, many issues came up. At first, Roosevelt did not respond to Republican charges, but he came back after them in sharp style toward the end of the campaign. One issue was the president's health; photographs showed how much he had declined between 1933 and 1944. The president's doctor assured the public there was "nothing organically wrong with him at all." A charge had been made that when the president visited Alaska, he had left his little Scotty dog, Fala, behind and had sent a navy ship to pick him up. In a speech, FDR answered the accusation. He said he and his family did not resent criticism, but Fala did. When Fala learned that so much money had been spent on him, "his Scottish soul was furious. He has not been the same dog since."

Dewey planned to charge Roosevelt with knowing, through the breaking of the Japanese code, that the attack on Pearl Harbor was coming. General Marshall sent a personal letter to Dewey asking that this not be used because the Japanese did not know their code was broken and were still using it. Out of patriotism, Dewey dropped the one issue that might have won him the election—that Roosevelt could have avoided the tragedy at Pearl Harbor but chose not to.

On election day, Roosevelt won 432–99 in electoral vote, 25.6 million to 22 million in popular vote. The new House was 242–190 Democratic, and the Senate 56–38 Democratic. The nation also had a new vice president who would become president on April 12, 1945, following the death of President Roosevelt.

Debate

In light of his poor health (which Roosevelt kept secret from the public), should he have run for office again in 1944?

Name_____ Date _____

POINTS TO CONSIDER

1. Should the health of the president be important in an election? Why?

_____

_____

_____

_____

_____

2. What were some reasons that unemployment dropped so rapidly during the war? How would that influence the way people voted?

_____

_____

_____

_____

_____

3. Most Americans knew very little about Truman in 1944. If you had been a voter at the time, why would you feel that more information was needed?

_____

_____

_____

_____

_____

Name _____ Date _____

CHALLENGES

1. Why is the opposing party limited in what it says about a president during a war?

_____

_____

2. Which party usually gains the most in off-year elections?

_____

3. Why did business leaders dislike Roosevelt?

_____

_____

4. How many seats in the House did Democrats lose after the 1942 election?

_____

5. How many fewer Democrats were there in the Senate after 1942?

_____

6. Did the 1944 economy favor the Democrats or the Republicans?

_____

7. Who was chosen as the Democratic candidate for vice president in 1944?

_____

8. According to Roosevelt, who resented the charge that he had wasted taxpayer money by sending a naval ship to Alaska?

_____

9. Who asked Dewey not to use the Pearl Harbor issue?

_____

_____

10. By how many popular votes did Roosevelt beat Dewey?

_____

_____

THE BATTLE OF THE BULGE

The invasion of France moved along well after D-Day, and many GIs in the U.S. Army were looking forward to sightseeing in Berlin within a few months. Watching planes fly overhead with bomb loads destined for German cities gave added confidence to men on the ground. But the war was not over, and the enemy showed signs of refusing to accept defeat. The landing at Antwerp, Belgium,

Although initially caught by surprise, Allied troops were able to force the Germans to retreat after the Battle of the Bulge.

had failed to provide the supply line that was needed because the Germans still controlled the approaches to the port. At Arnhem in the Netherlands, an Allied force was beaten back.

Hitler decided on a bold effort to break through the Allied line with a surprise attack through the Ardennes Forest. It was from the Ardennes that the Germans had attacked France in 1940; the plan this time was to drive toward Antwerp and split the Allied forces. The führer was excited as he made his plans and forced them on his reluctant generals, Rundstedt and Model. With the Allies defeated in the low countries, he could launch more V–2 attacks on London and weaken English support for the war.

The plans were devised in September, but Operation *Wacht am Rhein* (Watch on the Rhine) could not be carried out until December, when weather would hamper air support for the Allied armies. There were several problems with the plan. (1) The army brought together by the Germans to fight the battle included old men and the very young, as well as draftees from conquered regions, many of whom did not even speak German and certainly had no desire to die for the Third Reich. (2) Snow in the region was deep enough to stop a tank, and the forest was too thick for tanks to form a solid line for attack. (3) There was not enough fuel for the tanks. Unless they captured Allied supplies, the attack would literally run out of gas. (4) The attacking force had no reserves to fill in gaps in the line.

Civilian reports of tanks rumbling in the forest were ignored by Allied commanders who doubted that the Germans had enough resources for another offensive campaign. Allied troops in the region were either inexperienced or were combat men resting from other battles. On December 16, the *Panzers* came out of the forest and overran Allied positions. To succeed, the offensive had to take certain key points quickly.

One German drive was toward Spa, Belgium, where 3.5 million gallons of gasoline were stored. About 1 million gallons were removed before the Germans came. As the Panzers approached, 100,000 gallons were poured down the break they would be using and set on fire. Arriving U.S. tanks prevented any refueling stop at Spa. The Panzers then turned toward Trois Ponts where there was a bridge across the Ambléve River, but it was blown up as the Panzers arrived. Heading for another bridge, they found that it too had just been blown up. On December 18, that column of Panzers was spotted by low-flying planes, and troops were rushed to the area to block any advance.

Bastogne was a key town in the area road network, and both sides quickly saw its importance. More American troops were rushed in to prevent Bastogne from falling; the senior officer present was General Anthony McAuliffe. The Germans encircled the defenders during the night of December 21–22, and the Germans offered surrender terms to McAuliffe. Cut off and running out of supplies, McAuliffe replied with a one-word message, "Nuts!" The U.S. troops were saved by air drops on the 23rd and their commander's skill in artillery fire, which stopped one Panzer thrust after another. Patton's tanks arrived on the 26th to break the siege.

General Otto Skorzeny trained English-speaking German soldiers for Operation *Greif,* an interesting plot to confuse Allied troop movements and, if possible, to kill Eisenhower. Dressed in captured uniforms, seven jeeploads of Germans made it through the line. They did some damage in cutting telephone lines and sending troops down the wrong roads, but the greatest effect was caused by one who was caught and who said there were thousands of men in the unit. Americans began stopping those they did not know with questions like "Who is Mickey Mouse's girlfriend?" or "Who won the World Series last year?" These were questions the Germans had not prepared for. General Omar Bradley was stopped by a soldier asking: "What is the capital of Illinois?" He answered "Springfield." The soldier thought it was Chicago and asked who Bette Grable's husband was. The general did not know, but another soldier came, recognized Bradley, and let him go with the information that her husband was band director Harry James. The Germans who were captured were treated as spies and shot by firing squad.

Another surprise of the Battle of the Bulge was a gigantic *Luftwaffe* attack by 1,000 planes on New Year's Day. They destroyed 156 planes but lost 300. It was a costly attack since Allied planes could be replaced, but German planes could not.

By January 16, 1945, the bulge had ceased to exist, and the Germans were retreating to the West Wall. The battle had cost Germany 100,000 casualties, 800 tanks, and 1,000 planes. Hitler had again wasted resources in a battle he should never have fought.

Debate

Allied commanders were negligent in not expecting something like the Battle of the Bulge.

Name _____ Date _____

POINTS TO CONSIDER

1. Why would a less daring person not have considered the Wacht am Rhein?

_____

_____

_____

_____

_____

2. How did the failure to capture key points quickly affect the outcome of the battle?

_____

_____

_____

_____

_____

3. What questions would you ask that might separate a real American from someone pretending to be American?

_____

_____

_____

_____

_____

Name_____ Date _____

CHALLENGES

1. What two battles encouraged Hitler to think a counteroffensive might be useful?

_____

2. What name did Hitler give the new offensive?

_____

3. What was the German situation in regard to fuel supply?

_____

_____

4. What happened when the Panzers came close to the U.S. fuel depot at Spa?

_____

_____

5. What happened when the Panzers reached bridges crossing the Ambléve River?

_____

_____

6. What U.S. general was in command at Bastogne?

_____

7. What did the general at Bastogne say that made him famous?

_____

8. How were Germans in Operation Greif dressed?

_____

_____

9. What was the correct answer to the question, "Who is Mickey Mouse's girlfriend?"

_____

10. Who did not know the name of Bette Grable's husband?

_____

124

THE AIR WAR OVER GERMANY

In February 1945 Roosevelt and Churchill met Stalin at Yalta, in the Russian Crimea. That region had been held by the Germans, who had not only left destroyed tanks and trucks behind but looted and burned homes and other buildings of no military value as well. Other examples of Nazi cruelty were also coming in. German death squads had killed the wounded in the Battle of the Bulge and publicly ex-

Air raids on Germany were designed to weaken German support for war before ground troops moved in.

ecuted 22 civilians from Trois Ponts because U.S. soldiers had blown up their bridge. Victims of Japanese rule told of the abuse they had suffered. The leaders agreed that the Axis must be punished. No easy surrender terms were to let the enemy off lightly.

Air raids were a way to convince the enemy to surrender before they ever saw an Allied soldier or tank. The first air raid on Germany, on May 11, 1940, was a Royal Air Force (RAF) attack on Freiburg. At Casablanca, Roosevelt and Churchill agreed that the air war was to bring "the destruction and dislocation of the German military, industrial, and economic system and the undermining of the morale of the German people." The men in the RAF and U.S. Army Air Corps (AAC) were eager to accomplish those goals.

The RAF preferred attacking by night when it was safer. At the beginning of the war, the RAF had the Blenheim and Beaufort bombers, but as the war progressed, new bombers came out: the Whitley (1940), Wellington (1941), Mosquito (1941), Lancaster (1942), and the Halifax (1943). The British workhorse was the Lancaster. Protecting bombers were the fighters, the first of which were the Hurricane (1937) and Spitfire (1938). The Typhoon began replacing them in 1942. The Typhoon, at 400 miles per hour (mph), was the fastest RAF plane until the Meteor, a jet, came out in 1944, flying at 490 mph.

The AAC preferred day flying so that they could hit the target better. It benefited from U.S. mass production, which turned out planes of all kinds at a rapid pace. By 1943 U.S. factories were putting out 86,000 planes, and a year later, 96,000 planes. Some of these were being shipped to U.S. allies, but most were headed for the AAC or aircraft carriers in the Pacific.

Wars like the Second World War require an assortment of planes. The B–17 Flying Fortress went through many changes during the war. The B–17B came in 1939, the B–17G in 1944. A B–17G, fully loaded, had a 1,100-mile range with a 12,800-pound bomb load. The B–24 Liberator was a large plane with a heavy load capacity and long range. Unfortunately for its crews, it did not handle well, and one pilot considered it an "accomplishment to fly it [at all]." The B–26 Marauder was difficult to fly but was the medium bomber most used by the AAC. The B–29 Superfortress (1944) was the largest bomber in the war. Flying at 387 mph and heavily armed, the B–29 could carry heavy bomb loads. It was never used in

125

Europe, but Japan suffered from its attacks late in the war. None of these bombers were built with crew comfort as a high priority; they were cold, with tail and belly gunners stuffed in uncomfortable and cramped body positions.

Bombers needed fast-flying fighter planes with gas tanks large enough to fly the distance with them to protect them from pesky ME–109s. The best were not available until 1943 when both the P–47D Thunderbolt and P–38s came out; in 1944 the P–51D Mustang came out, and improvements continued to the P–51H model with a speed of 487 mph.

Out of the hundreds of bomber runs in Europe, certain raids stand out. In August 1942, an attack on the Ploesti oil refineries in Romania was carried out. The B–24s took off from Libya to attack the Nazi's major oil source. Reports said there were few antiaircraft guns there and that those were manned by Romanians. The reports were wrong. Hundreds of 88s and other machine guns and fast-firing cannons surrounded the refineries, with 50,000 Germans to fire them. Almost every disaster that could happen did. Ten of the 178 Liberators had to turn around because of sand in their engines. The lead navigator's plane crashed into the Mediterranean. A lead aircraft missed a checkpoint, and some other planes followed it to Bucharest. The lead plane of Colonel Addison Baker was a flying torch after it was hit, but he headed it straight toward the refinery where it blew up. Crews who later described the raid referred to it as a "trip through hell." The raid caused a short slowdown in Romanian oil production but cost 54 bombers.

The close support of their "Little Friends" (escort fighters) during a bombing run became important to the "Big Friends," the B–17s and B–24s. General Jimmy Doolittle, however, changed the role of the fighters from support to attack. His idea was to use the bombers as bait, force the *Luftwaffe* to come up after them, and shoot the "bandits" down when they arrived. If they did not come up, he wanted the fighters to strafe them on the ground. The targets for raids changed from aircraft production centers to cities sure to draw the Luftwaffe up to fight.

On March 6, 1944, the target was "Big B," Berlin, and one of the most brutal air battles of history followed. The AAC's 660 bombers and 800 fighter escorts tangled with 400 German ME–109s and FW–190s. The battle cost the AAC 69 bombers, but the Germans lost 80 fighters. Attacks on aircraft plants and on refineries producing high octane fuel, as well as losses in aerial combat, cut deeply into German air strength, but even more, they were losing their best pilots who could not be replaced. Antiaircraft guns continued to protect German cities, but the Luftwaffe no longer ruled the skies as it had in its glory years of 1939–1940.

Debate

Should cities or factories and refineries be the main targets for bomber attack?

Name _____ Date _____

POINTS TO CONSIDER

1. What part do you think air raids play in modern warfare?

_____

_____

_____

_____

_____

2. In a present-day war, what types of manufacturing might be considered the top priority for attack?

_____

_____

_____

_____

_____

3. How is air war the same and how has it changed since 1945?

_____

_____

_____

_____

_____

Name _____ Date _____

CHALLENGES

1. How did the setting at Yalta affect the leaders who met there?

_____

_____

2. What was the first German city attacked by air, and in what year was it attacked?

_____

3. What plane did most of the bombing for the British?

_____

4. Which two American bombers were hardest to fly?

_____

_____

5. Which was faster, the Meteor or the Mustang?

_____

6. What was the effect of the B–29 on the European war?

_____

_____

7. In AAC bombers, which crew members had the worst flying conditions?

_____

8. Why was Ploesti seen as an important target?

_____

_____

9. Who were known as the "Little Friends"?

_____

_____

10. What part of the German losses were impossible for them to replace?

_____

THE COLLAPSE OF NAZI GERMANY

If Hitler had been in his right mind, he would have realized that defeat was inevitable by January 1945. The noose was tightening, with U.S. and English forces coming from the west and Russians crushing his eastern flank. The stubborn generals who had bothered him with troubling reports were gone, killed by the enemy or by himself. A few generals were ignoring him, like the one who disobeyed orders to burn Paris, but turned the city over to the Resistance instead.

As Allied troops closed in on Germany, Hitler retreated to his underground bunker and killed himself.

A wiser leader would have realized that his army was too extended, to Greece and Italy on the south, Poland on the east, Norway on the north, and France on the west. Romania's very important oil fields had fallen in August 1944, at the same time that Allied troops were liberating northern France. In March 1945 U.S. troops found a bridge across the Rhine at Remagen that had not yet been demolished. Under heavy German fire, they crossed the bridge while the defenders were still trying to blow it up. U.S. troops were now on German soil and moving eastward to connect with the Russians. The Resistance was growing rapidly, and those who had been docile before were picking up rocks and grenades to use against Hitler's troops.

Planning the Battle of the Bulge restored some of Hitler's fighting spirit, but when it appeared the gamble might fail, he told his officers: "Never in my life have I accepted the idea of surrender." When General Guderian tried to warn him that the Russians were starting an offensive, he called the report nonsense. When the Russians came and his officers wanted to pull back, Hitler ordered them to hold their ground. The odds were too heavy against them and most surrendered. On January 30, 1945, with the Russian armies rolling over Hitler's army, Albert Speer told him that the war was lost.

By this time Hitler spent nearly all of his time in a bunker 50 feet below ground, under the Chancellery. There were two levels of the bunker: Hitler occupied three rooms on the lower level, his beloved Eva Braun had a bedroom and dressing room, and Joseph Goebbels stayed on the same lower level.

Speer had been with the führer almost from the beginning, but now was quietly resisting Hitler's demands for a scorched earth policy that would destroy not only factories, but houses, food supplies, and the transportation system. When Speer learned that special SS squads were being sent to enforce the order he was blocking, he provided machine guns to factory workers to protect themselves.

The drug-addicted Göring had lost much of his influence with the führer and his own *Luftwaffe*. By 1944 he was more of an art collector than a military and political leader. His offer to act as Hitler's successor on April 23 was seen as treason; he was arrested and stripped of his military rank and Nazi Party membership.

Mussolini tried to escape Italy dressed in a German uniform, but he was recognized, and partisans took him prisoner on April 28. He and his girlfriend were put up against a wall and shot. Their bodies were then taken to Milan and put on public exhibit hanging by their legs from meathooks. The large crowd threw stones and kicked the bodies.

In the early morning of April 29, Hitler learned that Himmler had made contact with the Swedes to try to arrange a peace settlement with the United States and Britain. Hitler turned purple with rage, and since he could not get his hands on Himmler, he had one of Himmler's aides shot instead. Hitler then wrote his last will and testament. He took no blame for failures or the murders of millions; he said he had been betrayed.

When a judge arrived Hitler married Eva Braun, who had been his secret lover for many years. Russian troops were moving into Berlin now, and Hitler was more afraid of them than of death. He located poison capsules, and after testing one that worked quickly on his loyal dog, Hitler made plans for his own death. At 2 P.M. on April 30, Hitler said his farewells to his staff, and he and Eva closed the door to his quarters. Hitler shot himself, and Eva took poison. Their bodies were taken out, soaked in gasoline, and then burned beyond recognition.

Goebbels tried to make peace with the Russians. When that failed, he poisoned his wife and children and then shot himself. Bormann somehow escaped and was never found alive. The West German government ruled in 1973 that a skeleton that had been found less than a mile from the bunker was Bormann's, but rumors persisted that he was alive somewhere. Himmler disguised himself as a low-ranking SS man, but was caught on May 21. While a British doctor was examining him on the 23rd, he swallowed poison he had hidden in a vial in his mouth.

Admiral Karl Doenitz had been left in charge by the führer, and he allowed as many Germans as possible to surrender to the U.S. and British troops. From the end of April to the first week in May, thousands of Germans crossed the Elbe River to reach the U.S. and British lines. General Jodl was sent to surrender on May 7 to the United States and on the 8th to the Russians. The war in Europe was officially over. The fascist rulers who had brought so much misery to millions of Europeans were gone. The Romans said it best: *Sic semper tyrannis* (Thus always to tyrants).

Debate

Do dictators always get the punishment they deserve?

Name _____ Date _____

POINTS TO CONSIDER

1. At what point in the war was defeat almost certain for Germany?

_____

_____

_____

_____

_____

2. If Hitler had lived and been brought before the war crimes judges at Nuremberg, what crimes might he have been charged with?

_____

_____

_____

_____

_____

3. Do you think the dictators ever understood how much they were hated?

_____

_____

_____

_____

Name _____ Date _____

CHALLENGES

1. What city was saved from destruction by a general refusing to obey Hitler's orders?

_____

2. What bridge was important to the U.S. invasion of Germany?

_____

3. How did Speer interfere with Hitler's orders?

_____

_____

4. What did Göring do that angered Hitler?

_____

_____

5. How did Hitler deal with Göring?

_____

_____

6. How did Mussolini die?

_____

_____

7. How did Hitler get revenge on Himmler?

_____

_____

8. How did Hitler die?

_____

_____

9. Which Nazi leader escaped?

_____

10. Who took over after Hitler's death?

_____

IWO JIMA AND OKINAWA

To battle-weary marines, the prospect of more island landings was nothing to look forward to. The Japanese had become masters of the art of island defense, just as marines had learned how to attack an island. Once again, it was a test of skills at Iwo Jima and Okinawa.

Iwo Jima was one of the most desolate islands imaginable. Made up of black, volcanic rock, its 1,500 caves provided great protection for its defenders, but that was not enough

Japanese troops hiding in pillboxes, tunnels, and caves were difficult for U.S. marines fighting on Pacific islands to flush out.

for General Kuribayashi, who put in pillboxes (small concrete enclosures for machine guns) and blockhouses with walls that were five feet thick. A tunnel network had also been added. Underground the sulphur was so hot that the men digging the tunnels could cook their rice on the sulphur wells in 20 minutes. The communications center was connected to the surface by a 75-foot-deep tunnel that was 500 feet long. The commander was determined that this island was not going to fall as Guadalcanal, Saipan, and the others had.

The importance of the island did not come from its scenic beauty or fertile soil. It came from its location. Only 760 miles south of Tokyo, Iwo Jima would make an ideal base for fighters that could escort B–29s on runs over the Japanese mainland. Marine officers looking at photographs of the island realized how dangerous their assignment was, and asked for ten days of heavy shelling by the Navy before starting their landing. The timetable allowed for only three days of naval attack, and on February 16 the ships began hitting all the known targets. Kuribayashi had ordered his men not to fire until the landing began, but a few got trigger-happy. When their gunfire was spotted, the *Nevada's* guns blasted them.

The landing began at 9:00 on February 19, and although ships and planes were dropping all kinds of missiles on them, the Japanese withheld their fire for the first hour. Then the Japanese guns started shelling the beach, and for the next 30 days, battles raged on the eight-square-mile island. There was high drama when six marines pushed a big flag between the rocks on the 550-foot-tall Mt. Surabachi. A photographer captured the event with a photograph that became one of the most famous of the war. Most of the battle for Iwo Jima was without glory. The Japanese were well dug in, and flame throwers, tanks, grenades, and bombs were needed to kill the defenders who were dishing it out as fast as they received it. A *kamikaze* attack was aimed at the ships offshore. The escort carrier *Bismarck Sea* was sunk, and the carrier *Saratoga* was badly damaged.

Nearly all of the island's defenders died; about 300 were killed in a *banzai* charge on March 21. Over 5,000 marines were killed and 20,000 wounded in the struggle. Admiral Nimitz said: "On Iwo Jima, uncommon valor was a common virtue." The island proved its value in the days ahead. B–29s, hit in raids over Japan, landed on the island or were picked up by sea planes from Iwo Jima. P–51s based there provided stronger air cover for the big

133

planes that were destroying Japan's cities and factories.

Lying between Formosa and Kyushu, Japan, is the 454-square-mile island of Okinawa. A narrow island, it is about 70 miles long and 2–16 miles wide. The island gets terrible rains, sometimes 11 inches in a day. Terrain in the northern part is very rugged; no one expected that the capture of Okinawa would be easy. General Ushijima had 100,000 troops on the island and hoped for air and naval support from the mainland. The U.S. force gathering to take the island was huge: 154,000 men in the attack force, with 1,400 ships to support them.

The softening-up process began in mid-March when carrier-based planes began attacking planes and airfields. This was costly; 116 U.S. planes went down, but they took out the Japanese planes on the island and damaged several ships. The Japanese responded with kamikaze attacks from Kyushu and hit five carriers, but only one was seriously damaged. The first landings took place on April 1 with little Japanese interference. By April 3, U.S. forces were across the island. Enemy resistance had been light at first; the troops knew this was too easy. Then came a swarm of 355 kamikazes from the mainland, aiming for the supply ships supporting the land forces.

The mighty *Yamato,* with its 18-inch guns, left port heading for Okinawa. All the fuel that could be found was put into this effort, and even then the *Yamato* did not have enough to return home. Only two escort planes went with it. A fleet of six battleships, seven cruisers, and 380 planes went out to meet it. The *Yamato* was a target 860 feet long and 128 feet wide at the beam. Planes had no trouble finding and sinking her. Half of the kamikazes were destroyed by U.S. planes, and 100 were hit by antiaircraft fire. Those getting through sank 36 small ships and damaged many others.

A mass counterattack on May 3 was planned by Colonel Cho and approved by General Ushijima. It called for an attack on the marines while kamikazes attacked the ships. The land attack was better planned than banzai charges, but the results were the same. Japanese casualties totalled 6,200 killed. At the same time, Japanese "Bettys" (the nickname for the OB–O1 torpedo bombers) attacked. Some had *bakas* (manned suicide rockets) attached to them. When the baka pilot spotted his target, he was released to do his job and sacrifice his life. Two destroyers were sunk and other ships damaged, but the Japanese lost 98 planes.

Despite heavy rains and Japanese resistance, the marines prevailed, and by the third week in June there was no hope for the defenders. Ushijima and Cho committed ritual suicide on June 22. Casualties were high for both sides. U.S. losses were about 49,000 including 7,000 killed on shore and 5,000 on ships. Japan lost about 100,000, with 10,000 taken prisoner.

Debate

An argument followed the battle because the navy had shelled the island for only three days instead of ten. Would shelling the island for more days have made much difference in the outcome?

Name _____ Date _____

POINTS TO CONSIDER

1. Why were land bases considered better than aircraft carriers?

_____

_____

_____

_____

_____

2. The *Yamato* was called a "suicide ship" for going to Okinawa. Why?

_____

_____

_____

_____

_____

3. "War of attrition" means that you wear the enemy down with your attacks and pressure. What problems did this tactic have at Iwo Jima?

_____

_____

_____

_____

135

Name _____ Date _____

CHALLENGES

1. Who set up the defenses at Iwo Jima?

_____

2. Why was Iwo Jima important?

_____

_____

3. How many days of softening by the navy did the marines want? How many did they get?

_____

4. What happened on Mt. Surabachi?

_____

_____

5. How many killed and wounded did the United States suffer at Iwo Jima?

_____

6. How much bigger (in square miles) was Okinawa than Iwo Jima?

_____

7. What was the difference between landing on Okinawa and landing the first day on Iwo Jima?

_____

_____

8. What happened to the *Yamato?*

_____

_____

9. Who was the Japanese commander on Okinawa?

_____

10. What were *bakas?*

_____

WEAPONS OF MASS DESTRUCTION

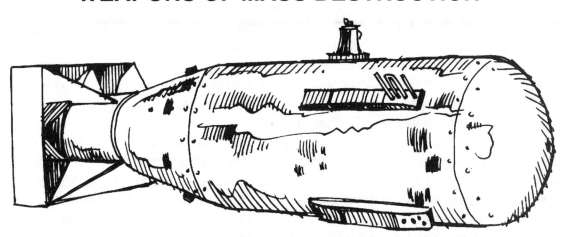

The atomic bomb would finally bring about the end of the war; however, it would bring with it the fear of misuse and mass destruction.

World War II was an example of the power of science. Radar had given the Allies a big advantage over the Axis from the beginning. Code-breaking machines let the Allies in on enemy secrets. The quality of Allied aircraft improved considerably while Japanese planes did not improve. If the Meteor and ME–262 had come out sooner, jets would have made the older planes obsolete. The edge went to the Allies in part because their enemies could not keep up with them in developing new weapons systems.

Scientific progress depends on a number of things: (1) the need for the product, (2) the financial backing for research and development, (3) scientists and inventors with the genius to take a concept and develop it, and (4) the technology to turn a blueprint into reality. It was the right combination of these elements that made the industrial, transportation, and communications advances of the 19th and 20th centuries possible. A war encourages development by creating an emergency situation that "jump starts" new advances, including the push for development of atomic energy.

In 1939 scientists in the United States and Europe were working on theories about creating a new form of energy through nuclear fission. British efforts were being speeded along by the presence of Jewish exiles from Nazi oppression and, later, by French scientists who escaped before their nation fell to the Germans. Important scientists were also coming to the United States: Enrico Fermi from Italy, Edward Teller and Eugene Wigner from Hungary, and Albert Einstein from Germany. Since Einstein was the best known, his help was needed to catch Roosevelt's attention. In a letter to the president, Einstein warned that a bomb using fissionable material would be very powerful, capable of blowing up a port and the area surrounding it. Some of the uranium the weapon required had been in Czechoslovakia, but the best source of uranium was the Belgian Congo.

At that point the Germans were ahead in the race. One of their scientists, Werner Heisenberg, was a leader in the field, and when they seized Norway in 1940, they took possession of the only heavy water (water containing deuterium that is used in the atomic process) factory in the world. German efforts did not produce a bomb because: (1) Hitler expected an early victory, (2) serious scientific problems were never solved, (3) German scientists were more interested in the V–1 and V–2 projects, and (4) the heavy water factory at Vemork, Norway, became a target for sabotage.

In a daring raid in February 1942, six Norwegian soldiers managed to get through the tight defenses at Vemork and blew up the plant, destroying a year's supply of heavy water. Bombing raids continued to keep production slow, and finally Hitler decided to close down the plant and take the 3,600 gallons of heavy water to Germany. Intelligence learned of this and, in another daring effort, sank the boat carrying the heavy water in the deepest waters of Lake Tinnsjö. That killed the German effort.

On December 6, 1941, Roosevelt decided to go all out to produce an atomic bomb. The development of the bomb was given the name "Manhattan Project" and was put under General Leslie Groves who was in charge of all army construction. The scientists disliked Groves because he expected them to obey his orders but did not understand the scientific problems facing the select group of Nobel prize winners he was dealing with.

One of the scientists, Dr. Arthur Compton of the University of Chicago saw that Groves was a man who could get things done and worked to calm the other scientists down. The place picked for the project was a squash court hidden away in the abandoned football stadium at the University of Chicago. The project was kept secret, and not even the university president knew that history was being made under his nose. Fermi led the team that produced the first self-sustained chain reaction on December 2, 1942. With that accomplished, creating a bomb was possible.

Two major plants were required for the project. Oak Ridge, Tennessee, and Hanford, Washington, were selected as sites to build the reactors and Los Alamos, New Mexico, for testing the finished product. The leader of the "eggheads" (Groves's name for the scientists) at Los Alamos was Dr. J. Robert Oppenheimer. Workers at Oak Ridge and Hanford had no idea what finished product would come from their plants. Even the scientists were under tight security regulations. Those working at Los Alamos were limited to 100-mile trips to Albuquerque, New Mexico, and their mail was censored. When the Los Alamos scientists protested, Groves drafted them into the army and put them in uniform. He wanted them to salute and stand at attention. The scientists refused, and Groves was finally forced to back down.

The U–235 produced in Oak Ridge was taken to Knoxville, transported to Chicago by train, and then taken west in a reserved train compartment to a station near Los Alamos. The test site was to be a desolate desert area Spanish explorers called *Jornado del Muerto* (Journey of Death); it was given the new name of Trinity. The bomb used for the test was named "Fat Man" because of its size and shape. At 5:30 A.M. the first atomic bomb exploded in the desert. A fireball 41,000 feet high rose in the sky. Observers were knocked down, the light was seen in Santa Fe, and people began to report the shock waves of a meteor falling, an earthquake, and an enemy attack. Only a few insiders knew what had really occurred.

Debate in 1944

Will the military and peacetime benefits of this project be worth the cost?

Name _____ Date _____

POINTS TO CONSIDER

1. Does war help or hurt scientific progress?

_____

_____

_____

_____

_____

2. Many of the scientists involved in the project did not believe in war. Why do you think they volunteered to join in the work?

_____

_____

_____

_____

_____

3. What differences do you see between a scientist's approach to problems and the army's approach?

_____

_____

_____

_____

_____

Name _____ Date _____

CHALLENGES

1. What machines had given clues as to what the enemy was up to?

_____

_____

2. What important scientist of the atomic project was Italian born?

_____

3. Where was Einstein born?

_____

4. What was produced at Vemork, Norway?

_____

_____

5. What happened when Hitler tried to remove the heavy water from Norway?

_____

_____

6. What was the program to develop a bomb called?

_____

7. Who tried to work out the differences between the scientists and the army?

_____

8. What nickname did General Groves give his scientists?

_____

9. How did Groves try to bring the scientists under closer control?

_____

_____

10. How high did the fireball rise in the experiment in the desert?

_____

ATTACKING THE JAPANESE MAINLAND

After the capture of Iwo Jima and Okinawa, it was only a matter of time until Japan was defeated. Like Southerners in the U.S. Civil War or Nazis in World War II, military reality seemed less important to the Japanese than the mindset that somehow good fortune

Regular bombings and napalm attacks destroyed large sections of Japanese cities and killed thousands.

would turn and victory could yet be won. Japan had hardly been touched, except by Jimmy Doolittle's raid early in the war, and many Japanese probably assumed that they were safe, but reality could no longer be ignored in 1944.

Attacks by air became a regular occurrence. B–29s based in China hit factories in Manchuria, Formosa, and Japan. The gasoline the planes needed, however, had to be flown up from India, so frequent missions could not be flown. By late 1944 the "Bees," as the Japanese people called the B–29s, were buzzing over Japan on a more regular basis. They came announced; planes were sent days in advance to warn the city that it was on the list to be hit, a suggestion to civilians that this was a good time to flee. It also demonstrated that the Bees were not afraid to let the Japanese air force know they were coming and were daring them to come up and fight.

A number of ideas were brought forward by Allied leaders about the best way to end the war. Military men involved in the Manhattan Project were convinced that an atomic bomb could convince the Japanese to give up. Some thought that if the Russians invaded Manchuria, the Japanese would realize that now the odds were overwhelming. The army was convinced that only an invasion of Japan would convince them to surrender. The navy thought that a blockade could stop the flow of oil and rubber to Japan. The air force wanted to continue the bombing that not only destroyed industry, but morale as well. The Joint Chiefs ordered that Japanese military and naval power be reduced by "unremitting pressure."

In the U.S. Civil War, General William T. Sherman said: "War is hell," and he wanted everyone in the regions where his army marched to know it. The planners of B–29 raids over Japan operated on the same philosophy. A warning to the city was enough, and those ignoring it were going to pay.

Napalm, an incendiary mixture, was General Curtis LeMay's weapon of choice. Japanese homes, made of paper and wood, made a napalm attack on a windy day especially effective. Japanese cities had very little protection from their fire departments, and once the fire was going, they could do little to stop it. Attacks on cities became common. The Bees came in low because of the strong winds at higher elevations. The March 8 raid on Tokyo killed 83,000 people and wiped out 16 square miles of the city. By the first week in June, Tokyo was 48 percent (32 square miles) destroyed, Osaka was 20 percent (8 square miles) desroyed, Nagoya was 10 percent (5 square miles) destroyed, and Kobe was 10 percent (3 square miles) destroyed. Other major cities attacked in fire bombings included Yokahama and Kawasaki, as well as 50 smaller target cities.

The crews of B–29s delivering the bombs ran many risks. They flew low to avoid radar and upper air currents, and that made the planes easy targets for anti-aircraft fire. The Japanese had a poor system of public warning that an attack was coming but were able to get a few planes in the air to attack their tormentors. One method used was ramming the B–29s, and they also began attacking from behind and flying upward to hit the plane's belly. With few fighters being produced, Japan decided to hide its planes away to save them for the invasion that everyone expected to come soon.

German defeat was almost certain by April, and the Japanese government was well aware of the devastating power of air attacks that had crippled its ability to make war. They had seen the fire bombing of their own cities, which had few defenses against the Bees that stung at will. Hope that the Russians would stay out of the Asiatic war began to disappear in April when the Japanese were informed that Stalin would not renew the Neutrality Pact with Japan. The Allies had told Germany to surrender unconditonally, but the Japanese leaders wanted terms that would allow them to save face and keep the emperor.

Some in power still thought Russia could be bribed to stay out of the war. "Give them Manchuria, and they will be satisfied," was their approach. When the Japanese ambassador in Moscow tried to sell that idea to the Russian foreign office, he was told that Stalin and Foreign Minister Molotov were preparing to leave for the Potsdam Conference.

At Potsdam President Truman was attending his first meeting with the leaders of Britain and the USSR. He had been informed about the results of the atomic bomb test at Trinity. In the middle of the summit, Churchill lost the general election in Britain and was suddenly replaced by the new prime minister, Clement Attlee. Most of the discussions at Potsdam were concerned with Europe, but Japan was not neglected. Japan's hope that Russia could be used to get them out of the war was in vain; Stalin intended to use the end of the war as an opportunity to seize land in Asia.

On July 26, 1945, Japan was told that the "unconditional surrender" of its armed forces was required; it would lose all of the territory that it had seized and be reduced to the four home islands. It would be occupied until it had a "peacefully inclined and responsible government." If Japan did not surrender, it would be destroyed.

Debate in 1944

Japan's civilians, if they do not heed the warning of a coming attack, are a legitimate target for bombing.

Name _____ Date _____

POINTS TO CONSIDER

1. Which of the tactics proposed by the army, navy, and atomic bomb supporters would have provided the quickest victory? The least costly (in lives) victory?

_____

_____

_____

_____

_____

2. How would a napalm attack on your city affect your determination to fight to the bitter end?

_____

_____

_____

_____

_____

3. The United States had been anxious to get Russia into the war against Japan. Why wasn't Truman as interested now? Why was Stalin more interested?

_____

_____

_____

_____

_____

Name _____ Date _____

CHALLENGES

1. Who made the only attack on Japan before 1944?

_____

2. Why didn't B–29s attack targets in Manchuria and Formosa more often?

_____

3. What were the "Bees"?

_____

4. How did the U.S. Army want to end the war?

_____

_____

5. How did the U.S. Navy want to end the war?

_____

_____

6. Why were napalm attacks especially successful in Japanese cities?

_____

_____

7. By June 1944 how much (%) of Tokyo was wiped out? How much of Osaka?

_____

8. What were three methods used by the Japanese to stop a B–29?

_____

_____

9. How did Japan hope to keep Russia out of the war?

_____

_____

10. What would happen to the Japanese Empire if Japan accepted the terms of the Potsdam Agreement?

_____

_____

THE WAR COMES TO A DRAMATIC END

The Japanese signed the treaty of surrender presented by American officers lead by General Douglas MacArthur September 2, 1945, on the U.S. battleship *Missouri*.

The warning coming from Potsdam that Japan must surrender or face total destruction was not a bluff. The mood of the Allies was obvious to the Japanese who saw their cities burning and their military capacity weakened with each new soldier killed, ship sunk, and plane shot down. Important decisions would have to be made by both sides.

In Japan, a heated argument followed the surrender demand. Foreign Minister Tojo spoke for those who thought surrender should be seriously considered, but Admiral Toyoda said that the declaration was absurd. They could only agree on letting newspapers publish it. One newspaper gave the editorial the headline "LAUGHABLE MATTER," and when Prime Minister Suzuki was asked about it, he said "We must *mokusatsu* it." He thought his remark meant the same as the English "no comment." The dictionary translates it as "ignore," or "treat with silent contempt."

Debate over the bomb had been going on in the United States as well. Acting Secretary of State Joseph Grew's suggestion that the Japanese be allowed to keep their emperor met with Truman's approval. Secretary of War Henry Stimson was thinking more about the effects of an atomic bomb, and he included three scientists on a committee to consider how it would affect political, military, and scientific questions. When Oppenheimer suggested that the bomb might kill 20,000 people, Stimson said the bomb should be used on military targets and that Kyoto (a beautiful, cultural city) was to be taken off the list. Dr. Arthur Compton wondered if a nonmilitary target could be found; this could show the Japanese the need to surrender without killing thousands of people. There were problems with that as well. If the bomb did not work or if the Japanese were not convinced, the effort would fail, and there were only two bombs in the arsenal. Oppenheimer and Fermi came sadly to the conclusion that "we can propose no technical demonstration likely to bring an end to the war; we see no acceptable alternative to military use."

Ignoring the bomb and going with an invasion of Japan had been ruled out. Estimates gathered by the army air force were that the Japanese had 14 divisions, 590,000 troops, and

7,000 aircraft to defend the mainland. This estimate was low; they actually had 710,000 troops and 10,000 planes. *Banzai* charges and *kamikaze* attacks had made it clear that an invasion of the Japanese mainland was going to cost thousands of American lives. General Marshall was most concerned about unnecessarily continuing the war when a quicker solution was available. The decision, after all the discussion, remained with President Truman. He never apologized for approving use of the atomic bomb.

On the island of Tinian, a bomb ten feet long and 28 inches in diameter waited for delivery on August 5. Only Colonel Paul Tibbets, captain of the B–29 *Enola Gay,* knew where it was being taken. Two days before, leaflets had been dropped on Hiroshima warning that the city was going to be wiped out unless Japan surrendered. At 8:15 A.M. on August 6, the *Enola Gay* flew over the city, and the bomb was released. The explosion was followed by a huge cloud rising over the city like a mushroom; minutes later, a black rain fell on those who survived.

In a short time, about 100,000 people had been killed, and thousands more suffered bad injuries and terrible burns.

The Japanese hope that Russia might help them was crushed on August 8 when their ambassador in Moscow was informed that the USSR was now joining the war against Japan. Two hours later, 1.6 million Russian troops crossed the border into Manchuria.

About 16 million new leaflets were dropped on Japan urging the people to petition the emperor to end the war, and "Evacuate your cities now!" On August 8 Major Chuck Sweeney took the pilot's seat on the *Bock's Car,* usually piloted by Captain Frederick Bock. Its atomic bomb was to be dropped on Kokura, but the city was covered with dense smoke, and the bombardier could not get a sighting. Running low on fuel, the pilot then flew to the secondary target, Nagasaki, where a break in the clouds made the target visible. The bomb exploded at 11:01 A.M. As in Hiroshima, death came quickly for some, more painfully and slowly for others. Loss of human life was again in the thousands.

Prime Minister Suzuki wanted to end the war as quickly as possible, but the army wanted to continue fighting. The argument was settled by Emperor Hirohito. Many army officers stubbornly wanted to continue the war and even dared refuse to obey an imperial decision. The main sticking point for the Japanese was the need for a guarantee that they could keep their emperor. On August 14 the United States informed Japan that they might keep the emperor if they chose but that he would take orders from the Allied supreme commander. The terms were acceptable to Hirohito, but many of his military leaders still wanted to continue the war. Some even attempted to prevent the emperor's speech to the nation, which had been recorded, from being delivered to the radio station.

Nearly all Japanese accepted the emperor's decision, but some did not and continued their own private wars. On September 2, 1945, the emperor's representatives boarded the battleship *Missouri* to sign an agreement of peace. After all papers had been signed, General MacArthur said: "Let us pray that peace now be restored to the world and that God will preserve it always."

Debate

Was dropping the atomic bomb the wise thing to do?

Name _____ Date _____

POINTS TO CONSIDER

1. If you were on the committee deciding whether or not to use the bomb, what would you have considered important in choosing a target?

_____

_____

_____

_____

2. What do you think banzai charges and kamikaze raids had to do with the question of whether to drop the atomic bomb or to invade?

_____

_____

_____

_____

3. Do you think Americans are as devoted to keeping a president as the Japanese were to keeping the emperor? Why?

_____

_____

_____

_____

Name_____ Date _____

CHALLENGES

1. What was Foreign Minister Tojo's attitude toward the Potsdam Declaration?

_____

_____

2. What did Admiral Toyoda think of it?

_____

_____

3. Which one did Prime Minister Suzuki seem to side with?

_____

4. How did Truman feel about letting the Japanese keep the emperor?

_____

_____

5. Why did Stimson want Kyoto taken off the list of targets?

_____

_____

6. Did the Japanese have more or less troops than the United States thought they did?

_____

7. What was the name of the plane that dropped the atomic bomb on Hiroshima?

_____

8. Why was Kokura lucky on August 8?

_____

_____

9. How did some army officers react when the emperor decided to surrender?

_____

10. What were the Japanese told on August 14 that made it easier for them to save face?

_____

_____

JUDGMENT DAY FOR WAR CRIMINALS

Nazis accused of war crimes were tried at Nuremberg, Germany.

At Yalta, Stalin had remarked that 50,000 Germans should be taken out and shot. Whether he was kidding or not no one knows, but Churchill was shocked by the statement and said that the English public would never allow such a massacre. It is estimated that 50 million people died in the war, many of deliberate starvation in concentration camps or at the hands of death squads. The innocent often suffer in war, but when cruelty becomes the official policy of a government, then a feeling of righteous indignation demands that the guilty be punished.

The subject of whom to punish was very complicated. There were many questions to be answered. Is a person who only obeyed the order of his superior a war criminal? If so every guard at Auschwitz was responsible for the genocide. Who would try a person who committed an atrocity in France, the French or an international court? Would it be fair to try a person for an offense that was not a crime when it was done? The U.S. Constitution forbids *ex post facto* trials, which means that a person cannot be punished for something done before a law was passed. Some felt that the United States should not get involved in the trials, but others pointed out that the Russians were less concerned about legal limits and might execute thousands or perhaps millions of Germans. Most puzzling of all was trying to define a war crime.

The trial for Nazi war criminals took place at Nuremberg, the site of early Nazi rallies. Defendants and groups (gestapo, SD, and so on) were tried for four types of offenses: (1) conspiring to use the Nazi Party to seize control of government in Germany, (2) crimes against peace (planning and carrying out wars of aggression), (3) war crimes (cruel treatment of civilians in occupied areas, plundering, and deliberate destruction of cities and towns of no military value), and (4) crimes against humanity (murder, enslavement, and persecution of political, racial, and religious groups).

The question of whether this was to be a trial or a lynching was settled when the elderly Gustav Krupp did not understand that he was accused of being a war criminal; doctors found that in his mental and physical condition he could not understand trial proceedings. The prosecutors admitted that defendants in their own country could not be tried if they were in Krupp's condition. His name was dropped from the list.

Of the Nuremberg defendants, twelve were sentenced to death, three to life in prison, two to 20 years, one to 15 years, and one to 10 years in prison. Three were found not guilty. Göring was sentenced to death but killed himself with poison. Rudolf Hess was the only inmate of Spandau Prison for many years, finally dying in 1987. Martin Bormann's whereabouts remained a mystery, but he was found guilty and sentenced to death *in absentia.*

Some of the "smaller fish" were tried in other courts. Josef Kramer, commandant at the Belsen concentration camp, was sentenced to death by a British military court. Those responsible for the conditions at Auschwitz were tried from December 1963 to August 1965. Punishment ranged from life at hard labor to three years and three months at hard labor.

Japanese accused of war crimes were also tried in United Nations courts. The accused were divided into three groups: CLASS A (those planning war in violation of international agreements), CLASS B (those violating the customs of war), CLASS C (those who carried out orders to torture or murder). These crimes were to go back to the 1931 invasion of Manchuria. No action was to be taken against the emperor. General Tojo was found guilty of war crimes and hanged in 1948. General Yamashita was tried in Manila, found guilty of war crimes, and hanged. General Homma, responsible for the Bataan Death March, was tried in Manila and executed by firing squad.

Some Axis leaders avoided the humiliation of a trial by committing suicide. Joseph Goebbels' last radio speech to the German nation on April 21 blamed the failure of the Third Reich on treason and cowardice. "Well, the venture has failed. . . . But when we depart, the earth shall tremble." On May 2 Goebbels poisoned his wife and children and then shot himself. Heinrich Himmler disguised himself in the uniform of an SS enlisted man, but was caught going through British lines. When a British doctor examined him, he found poison in his coat and ordered Himmler to put on an old British uniform coat. The doctor told his superior about the poison and was told to examine Himmler's mouth; he might have hidden poison there. When he came back, Himmler crushed a vial between his teeth and died minutes later. The earth did not tremble.

In 1941 Tojo had told his officers that death, even suicide, was better than surrender. War Minister Anami committed *hara-kiri* (ritual suicide) shortly before the emperor's surrender speech was broadcast. General Sugiyama, commander of home defense at the end of the war, committed suicide in September. Prince Konoye poisoned himself. Hundreds of other officers had killed themselves when their positions were overrun or they felt responsible for the loss of a battle. Now others who had killed or abused prisoners of war and civilians were killing themselves. Tojo tried to kill himself after he was captured but failed. He was criticized for not only doing a poor job of running the war, but bungling suicide as well.

Many "smaller fish" got away and were never found or were considered too unimportant to bother with. Some who escaped at the time were found later by Israeli Intelligence. One was Colonel Adolf Eichmann, who killed many Russian Jews. He was captured by the Israelis in Argentina in 1961 and taken to Israel for trial. Found guilty, he was hanged.

Debate

Should guards at concentration camps be held responsible for their cruel treatment of prisoners?

Name _____ Date _____

POINTS TO CONSIDER

1. What questions do you think should have been asked before Sergeant Wilhelm Schmidt (a fictitious name), a guard at Auschwitz, was brought to trial?

_____

_____

_____

_____

_____

2. What did the Krupp case show about the way judges wanted the trials to be conducted?

_____

_____

_____

_____

_____

3. The emperor of Japan was not tried because U.S. leaders knew it would cause too many problems with the Japanese people. Do you think that would have been an issue if Hitler had been captured alive?

_____

_____

_____

_____

_____

Name_____ Date _____

CHALLENGES

1. A Nazi was accused of crimes against Jewish prisoners in a concentration camp. Which charge was brought against him?

_____

2. A Nazi was accused of planning the invasion of Poland. Which charge was brought against him?

_____

3. A German officer was accused of destroying a small farm village. Which charge was brought against him?

_____

4. A Nazi was accused of plotting the overthrow of the democratic Weimar Republic in Germany. Which charge was brought against him?

_____

5. Why was Gustav Krupp not brought to trial?

_____

6. Who was the last remaining prisoner at Spandau prison?

_____

7. Who were three of the Japanese generals who were sentenced to death?

_____

_____

8. How did Goebbels escape trial?

_____

_____

9. Name three Japanese leaders who committed suicide.

_____

_____

10. What happened to Eichmann?

_____

_____

EFFECTS OF THE WAR ON WORLD HISTORY

On August 15, 1945, there was a general feeling of relief around the world as news of Japan's surrender was broadcast. It had been 14 long years since the Japanese invaded Manchuria, 6 years since German troops marched into Poland, and 4 years since Pearl Harbor. Some 50 million people had been killed, thousands of towns had disappeared from the map, and cities like Ber-

Fifty nations drew up and signed the United Nations Charter in the summer of 1945. The UN was organized to prevent threats to peace and develop friendly relations between nations.

lin and Tokyo were in ruins. The news of peace came none too soon. The inmate of the concentration camp was spared a cruel death, the prisoner of war (POW) was freed from his barbed-wire world. The GIs stationed in distant corners of the globe looked forward to their discharge and return to the "good old U.S. of A." Many Russian soldiers did not want to return, and when POW camps were overrun by U.S. and British troops, many Russian prisoners begged to stay. German and Japanese troops faced a grim future. They had marched to war as heroes in new uniforms; they returned in rags.

Many hoped that this would be the last major war to afflict their nation or the world. Roosevelt, a great admirer of Woodrow Wilson, wanted to create an improved version of the League of Nations. The term United Nations (UN) was first used in 1941 to include all nations at war with the Axis. In 1944 top diplomats of the major Allied nations met and recommended a United Nations Organization to prevent threats to peace and to develop friendly relations between nations. On April 25, 1945, the first formal meeting of the UN was held in San Francisco. The UN's success depended on good relations between the major powers, because they each had a veto power in the Security Council. The General Assembly was composed of delegates from all member nations. Problems came early to the UN when Russia began vetoing Security Council resolutions and, later, boycotting meetings.

Wars have a humpty-dumpty effect; once the egg breaks, its shell is never the same again. Consider the war's effect on EUROPE. In Eastern Europe, Communists replaced Fascists. Stalin wanted "friendly" governments in the region and used his power to force communist governments on East Germany, Poland, Hungary, Romania, and Bulgaria. At Yalta it had been agreed that Germany and Austria were each to be divided into four zones (United States, English, French, and Russian). In the western parts of Germany and Austria rebuilding began, but in the Russian zones conditions were very bad, and many fled to the nearest Western zone.

Communists threatened Greece after the war. The British tried to prop up its unpopular royal government. Russian eyes were also on Turkey because it controlled the channel into the Black Sea. The United States responded to both threats with the Truman Doctrine,

153

which offered military and economic aid to nations threatened by communist expansion.

Western Europe needed rebuilding, but its money had been spent on the war. The United States saw the need and began sending foreign aid. In 1947 a more systematic approach came with the Marshall Plan, which Secretary of State George Marshall described as an attack on hunger, poverty, desperation, and chaos. The United States put $13 billion into that effort alone.

In the MIDDLE EAST a homeland for Jews was established in Palestine, and the nation of Israel became a reality in 1947. Israel's neighbors were hostile from the beginning, and wars and border clashes were common. Pro-Axis threats developed in Iran and Iraq during the war, and the British moved troops into Iraq. The Russians and British moved into Iran. After the war the foreign troops were removed, and the shah was allowed to rule again.

ASIA. Japan went through major changes after the war. General MacArthur demanded some changes: women were given the vote, and Japan's armed forces were limited to defense only. Japan built up its industrial power and in a few years was among the greatest in the world. China's troubles were far from over, and the departure of the Japanese marked renewed conflict between Nationalists and Communists. India became independent, and the Muslim regions of India separated to form Pakistan in 1947. The Dutch East Indies became Indonesia. Nationalism developed in French Indochina, and this led to war against the French and, in time, the United States.

AFRICA. Like other colonial people, Africans wanted freedom from European rule. While it did not come as quickly there, it usually came more peacefully. In 1945 there were only four independent African nations. In 1960, 18 more nations joined that list, including 13 former French colonies. Today, there are over 50 free African nations.

The UNITED STATES came out of the war without the property damage and civilian casualty lists that affected most of the world north of the equator. The Depression era was gone, and Americans approached the future with a new self-confidence.

The war caused minority groups to be more assertive than in the past. The backbone of the civil rights movement was made up of blacks who had fought for democracy abroad and now demanded it at home. Women returned to homemaking, but Rosie the Riveter's image reminded them of that time between 1941 and 1945 when they were part of the blue collar workforce that won a war.

The long debate about whether the United States should take an active part in international affairs was not over, but presidents from Truman on took foreign policy issues very seriously. Neither party wanted the stigma of being "soft on communism," so defense, foreign aid (military and economic), and technical assistance programs were almost always passed.

From outer space the earth probably looked the same in 1945 as it had in 1939, but in the lives of its people dramatic changes had occurred. The world would never be the same again.

Debate

Was the world better or worse in 1950 than it had been in 1939?

154

Name _____ Date _____

POINTS TO CONSIDER

1. There were many hopes that the UN could prevent future wars. Do you think that it can prevent two major countries from going to war today?

_____

_____

_____

_____

_____

2. Why wasn't there a greater reduction of world tension after World War II ended?

_____

_____

_____

_____

_____

3. How did the war change the way Americans felt about themselves?

_____

_____

_____

_____

_____

Name_____ Date _____

CHALLENGES

1. What important event occurred on April 25, 1945?

_____

2. Where were the more powerful nations able to use a veto in the UN?

_____

_____

3. What part of the UN had representatives from all member nations?

_____

4. What were five nations that were dominated by Russia after the war?

_____

_____

5. What two nations were divided into four zones?

_____

_____

6. What two nations were helped by Truman Doctrine aid?

_____

_____

7. What new Middle East nation was born in 1947?

_____

8. What were two changes MacArthur required of Japan?

_____

_____

9. How many more African nations are free today than in 1945?

_____

10. How did the war affect American minorities?

_____

_____

REFLECTIONS ON WORLD WAR II

Writers have often noted the quiet of the battlefield after the last gun has fired: *Stillness at Appomatox* after the Civil War, *All Quiet on the Western Front* after World War I, and again in 1945, silence. There was a sigh of relief certainly. The concentration camp inmate had beaten the odds, the prisoner of war was released, the citizen of a conquered country looked forward to self-rule, the displaced person could return to his nation and home. The war had lasted too long for the 50 million who had died and had changed forever the lives of hundreds of millions of others.

After it was over, people began asking questions about why the war had happened, whether it could have been conducted better, and whether postwar problems could have been avoided.

HOW HAD IT BEGUN? Some say it is just human nature to fight, and wars are inevitable. They blame war on power struggles, greed, or arms races between the nations. Andrew Law wrote: "There is no such thing as an inevitable war. If war comes, it will be from failure of human wisdom."

Some blamed the war on the democracies that might have stopped the aggressors in their tracks at the beginning. When Japan invaded Manchuria, the Western nations only mumbled a protest. When Germans invaded the Rhineland, Austria, and the Sudeten, Hitler was bluffing, and there were some Germans who wanted to take him down. But no one called the bluff, and protesters became few and far between.

The major blame, however, must rest with those who conquered without regret and ruled without mercy. Dictators use any means to keep control and remove anyone who stands in the way. In fact, Hitler could have been far more successful if he had used common sense in ruling conquered people. If he had not used captive people for forced labor, cut food rations below the bare minimum needed for survival, used corrupt and evil Nazis, and destroyed the Jews and other "subhuman" neighbors, he might have been seen as an acceptable alternative to self-rule in some countries.

157

Americans also wondered how the United States had become involved in another world war. After all, public opinion polls up to November 1941 indicated that people were willing to send aid but did not want to fight. Despite neutrality acts that tried to prevent actions leading to war, the United States was fighting by December 1941. Many still believed that Roosevelt had created situations almost certain to force the Axis to attack. In their minds the blunders at Pearl Harbor were just too obvious to have been accidental.

HOW THE WAR WAS CONDUCTED raised many questions. Secretary of the Navy Frank Knox said: "Modern warfare is an intricate business about which no one knows everything and few know very much." In other words, plans on a map seldom work out as expected. Millions of lives were wasted in this war by Stalin and the Axis. They continued shellings long after cities were defenseless and strafed refugees along the roadways. Prisoners of war, supposedly protected by the Geneva Convention, suffered from bad food and poor medical treatment. Some of the worst wastes of life were of their own people. Hitler sent young boys out to die when the war was lost and refused to let his generals withdraw to better defensive lines. Stalin wasted millions of Russian lives by his lack of preparation. A Russian general at Leningrad said: "The stunning blows of the enemy caught our troops by surprise. We were not ready for battle." Stalin ignored the terrible losses of his own people. Japanese officers who ordered *banzai* charges and *kamikaze* flights had little concern for their men.

American generals made a definite effort to keep their troop losses down. They used bomber runs to soften the enemy. The medical treatment was much superior to that in any previous war. Prisoners of war in American and British hands considered themselves very fortunate. But after the war, serious questions were raised about why some casualties were victims of "friendly fire" (accidental attacks on friendly forces) and bombing raids that seemed motivated only by revenge. Lord Salisbury raised that same question in England: "Of course, the Germans began it, but we do not take the devil as our example."

Americans will long debate the decisions made about using the atomic bombs. Even if the bomb on Hiroshima was regarded as a military necessity, why wasn't more time allowed before the second bomb was dropped on Nagasaki? Was this a move to convince the Japanese to surrender, or to stop Russian expansion into Asia by demonstrating to Russia that the United States not only had the edge in weapons, but did not hesitate to use them?

WHY DID IT LEAVE SUCH A TANGLE OF PROBLEMS? Certainly that was not Roosevelt's wish. He remembered too well the failures of Versailles and had tried to avoid them. He had pushed hard for the United Nations Organization. At Yalta he tried to work out details of peace with Churchill and Stalin. Despite all efforts, so many problems remained when Truman became president on April 12, 1945, that he told reporters: "Did you ever have a cow fall on you?" Many "cows" fell on Truman in the next few years. Issues at home and overseas had to be dealt with: bringing U.S. troops home, converting to a peacetime economy, starting the UN, using the atomic bomb, ending the war, helping starving people, and aiding refugees returning home. Within two years, the United States and Russia were on the road to the Cold War and the possibility of World War III.

Before he died Roosevelt finished a speech that he intended to give on Jefferson's birthday (April 13). He wrote: "Today, we are faced with the preeminent fact that, if civilization is to survive, we must cultivate the science of human relationships—the ability of all peoples, of all kinds, to live together and work together, in the same world, at peace."

ANSWERS TO CHALLENGES

The Legacy of Versailles (page 4)
1. Wilson: "World must be made safe for democracy," and "war to end all wars."
2. Weapons: submarine, airplane, machine gun, poison gas.
3. List: Fourteen Points.
4. Representatives: Georges Clemenceau (Fr) and David Lloyd George (GB).
5. Regions: Alsace-Lorraine permanently; for 15 years, Saar.
6. Name: Weimar Republic.
7. New nations: Austria, Hungary, Czechoslovakia.
8. Austria: could not join Germany.
9. Article X: members to protect each other from external aggression.
10. Article XVI: use economic and financial boycotts against violators of Covenant.

The Rise of Dictators (page 8)
1. Naval conference: aircraft carriers and capital ships.
2. Kellogg-Briand Pact: discard war as national policy.
3. Wars: involved whole populations, and fought with all available means.
4. Dictatorship: all power in hands of one person or small elite group.
5. Agency: Comintern.
6. Nations: China, Russia, Korea.
7. When: 1932.
8. Battle: Socialists.
9. Black Shirts: Fascist squads.
10. Matteotti's death: don't criticize Fascists.

Nazi Germany (page 12)
1. Sparticists: no.
2. Houses: *Reichstag* and *Reichsrat.*
3. Name: National Socialist.
4. Groups: Jews and Communists.
5. SA: Brown Shirts.
6. Groups: liberals, Jews and Bolsheviks (Communists).
7. Seats: 218.
8. Problem: Hitler needed the support of industrialists and aristocrats.
9. Solution: Rohm and 200 SA executed.
10. Concentration camps: Dachau and Buchenwald.

The Winds of War Begin to Blow (page 16)
1. Excuse: explosion on South Manchurian Railroad.
2. Name: Manchukuo.
3. Prevented: Mussolini.
4. Weapons: spears and arrows.
5. Violation: Treaty of Versailles and Locarno Pacts.
6. French: German forces would have withdrawn.
7. Involved: France and Russia, Germany and Italy.
8. Agreement: Anti-Comintern Axis.
9. *Anschluss*: Germany and Austria.
10. Excuse: Germans in Sudeten were suffering.

The Opening Salvos of World War II (page 20)
1. Leader: Mao Zedong.
2. Cities: Shanghai and Nanjing.
3. Reason: they had warned that attack meant war.
4. Reason: they knew Polish soldiers had not been involved in the raid.
5. Waves: air and armor.
6. Line of defense: Maginot Line.
7. French odds: yes.
8. Name: sitzkrieg.
9. Helped: underground activities of Quisling.
10. Fame: because 337,000 troops were rescued there in 1940.

The War Spreads (page 24)
1. Supplies: left behind at Dunkirk.
2. Russians: 1 million.
3. Tojo: French Indo-China (Vietnam).
4. German: *Luftwaffe, Wehrmacht,* and *Panzer.*
5. Göring: attack shipping, the RAF, and cities.
6. August 13: day that the Battle of Britain began.
7. England: Hurricanes and Spitfires; Germans: ME−109 and ME−110.
8. Planes: 34.
9. Importance: Germans called off Sea Lion.
10. U.S.: leases on naval bases.

Two Giants Enter the War (page 28)
1. Bankers: belligerents could not borrow.
2. *Lusitania*: U.S. ships could not carry munitions to belligerents.
3. Conquered: France, Denmark, and Netherlands (or Dutch).
4. Defense: Canada.
5. Similar: neighbor with house on fire.
6. Tried: Napoleon.
7. Purpose: invade Russia.
8. Ships: *Greer, Kearny, Reuben James.*
9. Japanese ships: 31.
10. Leaders: Yamashita and Yamamoto.

Goliaths Fall to Slingshots: The Naval War (page 32)
1. Mitchell: submarine, submarine.
2. Nation: Uruguay.
3. Ships: *George V* and *Rodney.*
4. Ready: 7.
5. Air cover: *Indomitable* had been damaged.
6. Goals: hold Hawaii and keep communication with Australia open.
7. Sunk: 2.9 ships per day.
8. Deck guns: to save torpedoes.
9. Codes: Enigma and Purple Code.
10. Name: Coastal Picket Patrol.

Losing and Winning Some in the Pacific (page 36)
1. Countries: China, Malaysia, Burma, teacher acceptable answer.
2. Route: Burma Road.
3. Nickname: Aluminum Trail.
4. Positions: Bataan and Corregidor.
5. Quote: Douglas MacArthur.
6. Raid: Jimmy Doolittle.
7. Died: 17,000.
8. U.S. carrier: *Lexington.*
9. Coral Sea: neither fleet saw nor shot at each other.
10. Japanese carrier: *Hiruyu.*

The German Advance to the Gates of Moscow (page 40)
1. Hitler: "unmerciful and unrelenting harshness."
2. Military: political commissars watching them.
3. Voronav: disagreed with Beria over artillery.
4. Rokossovsky: teeth knocked out by NKVD (secret police).
5. Animals: reindeer, horses, dogs.
6. Tanks: T–34 and planes: Yak–1M.
7. Distance: 15 miles.
8. Attacked: supply and ammunition trucks.
9. Groups: women, children, elderly.
10. Production: 10,700 planes, 14,300 tanks.

The Nazi Nightmare at Stalingrad (page 44)
1. Stalingrad: tanks, steel, and small arms.
2. Commanders: Manstein and Paulus.
3. Importance: tied down German troops that could have been sent to Stalingrad.
4. Rundstedt: failed to capture Moscow.
5. Leaders: Zhukov, Rokossovsky, Heremenko, Chuikov, and Khrushchev.
6. Luftwaffe: created rubble for Russians to hide behind.
7. Supply: Göring.
8. Tried: Manstein.
9. Rank: field marshal.
10. Losses: 300,000.

The Afrika Korps Reaches El Alamein (page 48)
1. Colony: Ethiopia.
2. Tobruk: Mediterranean.
3. Air raids: 1,600.
4. Maltese survived by hiding in caves.
5. Army: Afrika Korps.
6. Trained: overheated barracks, limited water, and created artificial sandstorms.
7. Nickname: Desert Fox.
8. Officers had to run seven (later six) miles a week.
9. Sapper: lays or disarms mines.
10. Army: British.

A "Torch" Lights in North Africa (page 52)
1. Churchill: help British at El Alamein.
2. U.S.: still had diplomatic ties.
3. De Gaulle: leader of Free French.
4. Murphy: contacted anti-Nazi French officers.
5. Clark: hid in cellar during police raid.
6. Darlan: Commander in chief of Vichy France.
7. Replaced: Henri Giraud.
8. Tedder: English, helped coordinate air and ground operations.
9. Battle: Kasserine Pass.
10. Rommel: in Berlin; 275,000 surrendered.

The Arsenal for Democracy (page 56)
1. Phrase: Roosevelt.
2. Government in WW I took control of food, production, railroads, labor relations, and public opinion.
3. Business: Secretary of War Henry Stimson.
4. Tradition: baseball, movies, and Broadway shows.
5. Cars: War Production Board (WPB).
6. Gas: Office of Price Administration (OPA).
7. Groups: unions, farmers, landlords, and those unhappy over rationing.
8. Clothes: Office of Scientific Research and Development (OSRD).
9. Planes: 90,462.
10. Fastest: 14 days.

American Women in the War (page 60)
1. War: Civil War.
2. Clerks: Yeomanettes.
3. Post: OK if used work badge, but not thumb.
4. Wage: 60¢ an hour.
5. Group: American Women's Voluntary Services (AWVS).
6. Entertained: United Services Organization (USO).
7. Army: WACS (earlier WAACS).
8. Navy: WAVES.
9. Excuse: women too high strung.
10. Mrs. Roosevelt: women wanted to contribute to war effort.

America's Minorities in the War (page 64)
1. Louis: didn't think Hitler would fix problems.
2. Aviators: Tuskegee, Alabama.
3. Action: 761st Tank and 614th Tank Destroyer Battalions.
4. Discrimination: race, creed, color, or national origin.
5. State Department: thought it might hurt relations with Latin America.
6. Germans and Italians: travel restrictions, and could not own shortwave radios, maps, or guns.
7. Differences: *Issei* born in Japan, *Nisei* in United States.
8. Executive Order 9906: authorized relocation camps.
9. Black: war creates hardship; when in danger, must respond to threat.
10. Roberts: questions of loyalty and disposition (attitude) toward the United States.

Life Under the Third Reich (page 68)
1. Hess: Deputy führer.
2. Goring: Reichmarshall of the Luftwaffe.
3. Propaganda: Joseph Goebbels.
4. Decided: Martin Bormann.
5. Obedience: Hitler was leader of the master race.
6. Organizations: HJ and DJ.
7. Poles: taken from parents and given to German families.
8. Food: France, Belgium, and Holland.
9. Danes: made jokes at German expense.
10. Poles and Ukranians: seen as subhumans.

The Final Solution Spreads (page 72)
1. Russia: pograms.
2. City: Frankfurt, 4 percent.
3. Professions: lawyers, brokers, doctors.
4. Complaint: Jews had protested to outsiders about how they were treated.
5. Left: Thomas Mann and Albert Einstein.
6. Added: Israel or Sarah.
7. Pressure: lifted because of Berlin Olympics.
8. Name: because of shattered glass on streets.
9. Solution: death of all Jews.
10. Agency: SS or RSHA.

The Island War in the Pacific (page 76)
1. Continent: Australia.
2. Percent: 30 percent.
3. Title: Supreme Commander of the Southwest Pacific Area.
4. Navy: Chester Nimitz.
5. Marine: Alexander Vandergrift.
6. *Banzai:* 10,000 years. Meant the person was willing to die for the emperor.
7. Unofficial name: Operation Shoestring.
8. The Slot: supply line for Japanese soldiers on Guadalcanal.
9. Town: Port Moresby, 30 miles.
10. Civilians: jumped off ledge into the ocean.

Marshall's Team in Europe (page 80)
1. Characteristic: performance.
2. Patton: benched him, but brought him back when he was needed.
3. Assignment: War Planning Office.
4. Method: put U.S. and British officers across from each other, so each knew what others were doing.
5. Bulldog: Beadle Smith; Churchill.
6. Bradley: regarded highly by his men.
7. Patton: tanks.
8. Pershing: fighter who is so bold he is dangerous.
9. Battles: fastest and hardest-hitting armies.
10. Clark: long nose.

The Invasion of Sicily and Italy (page 84)
1. Italians: saw Americans as liberators, not conquerors.
2. Pantelleria: quickly surrendered.
3. LST carried men, LCT carried tanks and artillery.
4. Reason: Germans on west coast.
5. Sicily: 11 days.
6. Mussolini: denounced, fired, and arrested.
7. Patton: slapped soldier with glove.
8. Punishment: had to apologize to the men and every unit in his army.
9. Reaction: sent troops to rescue him.
10. Italians: 3.5 ounces of bread a day.

Struggling Against Men and Mountains in Italy (page 88)
1. Mountains: Apennines and Matese.
2. Defense: Gustav and Gothic lines.
3. October 13: Italy joined war on Allied side.
4. Person: Churchill.
5. Leader: John Lucas; Alban Hills.
6. Rapido: Fred Walker; it failed.
7. Freyburg: believed Germans using it.
8. Clark: it would create rubble for the Germans to use.
9. Rome: Normandy invasion.
10. Invasions: southern France and Greece.

Allied Leaders Develop Grand Strategies (page 92)
1. Roosevelt: like field general fighting on many fronts.
2. Group: America First.
3. Continents: Asia, Africa, and Europe.
4. Job: journalist, opposed them.
5. Goal: victory.
6. Result: Atlantic Charter.
7. Declaration: called for united front against Axis, with no separate peace treaties.
8. Stalin: so Russians and Germans could kill each other off.
9. Promise: to fight until Japan's unconditional surrender.
10. Second Front: Russia would open an offensive at same time.

Preparing for D-Day (page 96)
1. Supplies: defense.
2. Timing: offense.
3. DeGaulle: ties to French Resistance.
4. Rommel: command of coastal defenses.
5. Schweppenburg: protect tanks from naval artillery.
6. Targets: Eisenhower: transportation; Spaatz: refineries and aircraft plants.
7. NORTH: make the Germans think Norway was to be invaded.
8. FORTITUDE: Patton.
9. Stagg: chief meteorologist.
10. Quote: Eisenhower.

D-Day Arrives (page 100)
1. Allies: bombed radar stations, cut phones, and bombed railroads.
2. Storm: grounded Luftwaffe, kept navy in harbor, and caused defenders to relax.
3. Devices: balloons and aluminum foil.
4. City: Omaha; state: Utah.
5. Time: 5 hours, 19 minutes.
6. Reason: Rundstedt had ordered reserves up without permission.
7. Area: 50 miles.
8. Men: 150,000 and ships 5,300.
9. Nicknames: buzz bombs and doodle bugs.
10. Plane: ME–262.

Efforts to End the Hitler Era (page 104)
1. Dislike: because they wanted to show they were masters.
2. Group: SOE (Special Operations Executive).
3. Method: BBC radio broadcasts.
4. Saved: Dr. Martin Niemöller.
5. Pope Pius XI: exposing Catholics to illegal and inhuman violence.
6. Bishop: Cardinal Galen.
7. Nazis: brought false charges against him.
8. Plot: General Beck.
9. Reason: he heard the explosion and saw the roof cave in.
10. Found guilty: 7,000.

Concentration Camps: Centers for Genocide (page 108)
1. Holocaust: great or complete devastation or destruction.
2. Genocide: to kill an entire group.
3. German Jews: to Polish ghettos.
4. Crime: death of Heydrich.
5. Doctor: Mengele.
6. Sign: "Work Brings Freedom."
7. Auschwitz: 12,000 per day.
8. Maidanek: 1.5 million.
9. Watches: given to SS and wounded soldiers.
10. Denmark: 90 percent.

The U.S. Navy's Turkey Shoot (page 112)
1. *Indianapolis*: cruiser.
2. *Missouri*: battleship.
3. *Saratoga*: aircraft carrier.
4. *Starfish*: submarine.
5. Aircraft: Hellcat and Corsair.
6. Floater: surface mine.
7. Kills: *Tautog*, 26.
8. Ships: U.S., 112; Japan, 55.
9. Carriers: 5
10. Lost planes: 395.

Liberating the Philippines (page 116)
1. Yamamoto: Bougainville.
2. Carriers: 19, 0.
3. Statement: "I shall return."
4. Shima: saw U.S. fleet intact.
5. *Kamikazes:* young men.
6. Missions: 1.
7. Losses: Japan 11, U.S. 4.
8. Manila: Luzon.
9. Reason: Japanese troops pulled back into interior.
10. Surrender: September 2, 1945.

The Unusual Politics of Wartime Elections (page 120)
1. Party: doesn't want to seem unpatriotic.
2. Gains: party out of power.
3. Leaders: thought Roosevelt favored labor too much.
4. House: 50 seats.
5. Senate: 6 seats.
6. Favored: Democrats.
7. Vice president: Harry Truman.
8. Resented: Fala.
9. Pearl Harbor: Marshall.
10. Margin: 3.6 million.

The Battle of the Bulge (page 124)
1. Battles: Antwerp and Arnhem.
2. Name: *Wacht am Rhein* (or Watch on the Rhine).
3. Fuel: short supply, and needed to capture Allied fuel to continue.
4. Spa: 100,000 gallons set on fire.
5. Ambléve: bridges blown up.
6. Bastogne: Anthony McAuliffe.
7. Statement: "Nuts."
8. Dressed: U.S. Army uniforms.
9. Answer: Minnie Mouse.
10. Didn't know: Omar Bradley.

The Air War Over Germany (page 128)
1. Yalta: made them determined to win total victory.
2. City: Freiburg, 1940.
3. RAF: Lancaster.
4. Hardest to fly: B–24 Liberator and B–26 Marauder.
5. Faster: Meteor.
6. B–29: no effect, wasn't used in Europe.
7. Crew: belly and tail gunners.
8. Ploesti: its oil refineries supplied much of Germany's oil.
9. Little Friends: fighter escorts.
10. Losses: best pilots.

The Collapse of Nazi Germany (page 132)
1. City: Paris
2. Bridge: Remagen.
3. Speer: blocked orders for mass destruction.
4. Göring: offered to act as Hitler's successor.
5. Hitler: had Göring arrested and took away his military rank and party membership.
6. Mussolini: put against wall and shot.
7. Hitler: executed one of Himmler's aides.
8. Hitler shot himself.
9. Escaped: Martin Bormann.
10. Took over: Karl Doenitz.

Iwo Jima and Okinawa (page 136)
1. Defenses: Kuribayashi.
2. Importance: 760 miles from Tokyo, could be used as airbase.
3. Asked: 10 days, got 3 days.
4. Surabachi: U.S. flag planted there.
5. Total: 25,000.
6. Size: 446 more square miles.
7. Difference: less resistance on Okinawa.
8. *Yamato:* was sunk.
9. Commander: Ushijima.
10. *Bakas:* suicide rocket planes.

Weapons of Mass Destruction (page 140)
1. Machines: radar and code breakers.
2. Italian: Enrico Fermi.
3. Einstein: Germany.
4. Vemork: heavy water.
5. Water: boat sank in Lake Tinnsjö.
6. Program: Manhattan Project.
7. Work out differences: Dr. Arthur Compton.
8. Name: eggheads.
9. Groves: tried to draft them into army.
10. Fireball: 41,000 feet in air.

Attacking the Japanese Mainland (page 144)
1. Early attack: Jimmy Doolittle.
2. Targets: because gasoline had to be brought across the mountains.
3. Bees: B–29s.
4. Army: Invasion.
5. Navy: blockade.
6. Napalm: cities made with wood and paper houses.
7. Tokyo, 48 percent; Osaka, 20 percent.
8. Methods: ramming, attack from tail or under belly.
9. Russia: offer them Manchuria.
10. Potsdam: Japan would be reduced to four home islands.

The War Comes to a Dramatic End (page 148)
1. Tojo: thought it should be taken seriously.
2. Toyoda: thought it was absurd.
3. Suzuki: remark seemed to side with Toyoda.
4. Truman: approved.
5. Stimson: said Kyoto was beautiful, cultural center and had no military value.
6. Troops: more.
7. Plane: *Enola Gay.*
8. Kokura: lucky it had dense smoke cover or bomb would have been dropped there.
9. Officers: still wanted to continue the fight.
10. Term: allowed to keep the emperor.

Judgment Day for War Criminals (page 152)
1. Concentration camp: Charge 4.
2. Poland: Charge 2.
3. Village: Charge 3.
4. Weimar: Charge 1.
5. Krupp: could not understand charges.
6. Spandau: Rudolf Hess.
7. Generals: Tojo, Yamashita, and Homma.
8. Goebbels: shot himself.
9. Leaders: Anami, Sugiyama, and Konoye.
10. Eichmann: escaped to Argentina, caught in 1961 by Israel and executed.

Effects of the War on World History (page 156)
1. Event: first formal meeting of the UN.
2. Powerful: Security Council.
3. All members: General Assembly.
4. Five dominated nations: East Germany, Poland, Hungary, Romania, and Bulgaria.
5. Zones: Germany and Austria.
6. Truman Doctrine: Greece and Turkey.
7. New nation: Israel.
8. Japan: women allowed to vote, and military limited to defense only.
9. Africa: at least 46.
10. Blacks: demanded rights.

BIBLIOGRAPHY

There are thousands of books dealing with World War II, and those included here are only a small sample. Series of books such as Churchill's six volume set have been combined. It is suggested that the beginning student start with an encyclopedia, look at the bibliography at the end of the subject of interest, and begin a search for more information from there. Some students might also enjoy a visit to a library that has the magazines from that time, or magazines like *World War II,* which discuss the time period, and experience in that way the excitement and drama of the war years.

Series

Army Air Force in World War II.
Churchill, Winston. *The Second World War.* Cambridge, Massachusetts: Houghton-Mifflin, 1948.
The Epic of Flight. Alexandria, Virginia: Time-Life, 1982.
History of the U.S. Army in World War II.
Morison, Samuel E. *History of Naval Operations in World War II.*
World War II. New York: Time-Life, 1976.

General

American Heritage Picture History of World War II. New York: American Heritage, 1966.
Buchanan, A. Russell. *The United States and World War II.* New York: Harper & Row, 1964.
Calvocoressi, Peter and Guy Wint. *Total War: the Story of World War II.* New York: Pantheon, 1972.
Davis, Kenneth. *The Experience of War.* Garden City, New York: Doubleday, 1965.
Fuller, J.F.C. *The Second World War.* New York: Duell, Sloan & Pearce, 1962.
Keegan, John. *The Second World War.* New York: Penguin, 1989.
Weinberg, Gerhard. *The World at Arms.* Cambridge: Cambridge University, 1994.
Wheal, Elizabeth-Anne, Stephen Pope, and James Taylor. *A Dictionary of the Second World War.* New York: Peter Bedrick, 1990.

Autobiographies and Biographies

Ambrose, Stephen. *Eisenhower.* New York: Simon and Schuster, 1983.
Aron, Robert. *De Gaulle.* New York: Harper & Row, 1966.
Barnett, Correlli. *The Desert Generals.* Bloomington: University of Indiana, 1982.
Bradley, Omar. *A Soldier's Story.* New York: Holt, 1951.
Browne, Courtney. *Tojo, the Last Banzai.* New York: Holt, Rinehart & Winston, 1967.
Bullock, Alan. *Hitler.* New York: Harper & Row, 1963.
Collier, Richard. *Duce! A Biography of Mussolini.* New York: Viking, 1971.
Eisenhower, Dwight. *Crusade in Europe.* New York: Doubleday, 1948.
Goebbels, Joseph. *Diaries.* New York: Putnam, 1978.
Hyde, Montgomery. *Stalin: The History of a Dictator.* New York: Giroux, 1961.
Lee, Clark and Richard Henschel. *Douglas MacArthur, Biography.* New York: Holt, 1952.
MacGregor-Hastie. *The Day of the Lion* [Mussolini]. London: MacDonald, 1963.
Mosley, Leonard. *Hirohito, Emperor of Japan.* Englewood Cliffs, New Jersey: Prentice-Hall, 1960.
Patton, George. *War As I Knew It.* New York: Houghton-Mifflin, 1947.
Pogue, Forest. *George C. Marshall, a Biography.* New York: Viking, 1963, 1965, 1973.
Rommel, Erwin. *The Rommel Papers.* New York: Harcourt, Brace, 1953.
Roosevelt, James and Sidney Shalett. *FDR.* London: Harrap, 1960.
Speer, Albert. *Inside the Third Reich.* New York: Macmillan, 1970.
Truman, Harry. *Memoirs, Vol. 1, Year of Decisions.* New York: Doubleday, 1955.

Topics

Belote, James H. and William M. *Typhoon of Steel: The Battle for Okinawa*. New York: Harper & Row, 1982.

Brackman, Arnold. *The Other Nuremberg* [Japanese war crime trials]. New York: Morrow, 1987.

Buchanan, A. Russell. *The United States and World War II*. New York: Harper & Row, 1964.

Conot, Robert. *Justice at Nuremberg*. New York: Harper & Row, 1983.

Daniels, Roger. *Concentration Camps U.S.A. : Japanese Americans and World War II*. New York: W.W. Norton, 1967.

Erickson, John. *The Road to Stalingrad*. New York: Harper & Row, 1975.

Fest, Joachim. *Hitler*. New York: Harcourt Brace Jovanovich, 1974.

Froman, James. *Code Name Valkyrie: The Plot to Kill Hitler*. New York: Phillips, 1973.

Fuchida, Mitsuo and Masadake Okumiya. *Midway: The Battle That Doomed Japan*. Annapolis: U.S. Naval Institute, 1955.

Hartmann, Susan. *The Home Front and Beyond: American Women in the 1940s*. Boston: Twayne, 1982.

Hastings, Max. *Overlord, D-Day, June 6, 1944*. New York: Simon & Schuster, 1984.

Heydecker, Joe and Johannes Leeb. *The Nuremberg Trials*. London: Heinemann, 1962.

Hogg, Ian. *The Great Land Battles of World War II*. New York: Doubleday, 1988.

Hosokawa, William. *Nisei: The Quiet Americans*. New York: William Morrow, 1969.

Kenney, William. *The Crucial Years 1940–1945*. New York: Macfadden, 1962.

Leckie, Robert. *The Battle for Iwo Jima*. New York: Random House, 1967.

___. *Challenge for the Pacific: The Struggle for Guadalcanal*. New York: Doubleday, 1965.

Lord, Walter. *Incredible Victory, The Battle of Midway*. New York: Harper & Row, 1967.

Mauldin, Bill. *Back Home*. New York: William Sloan, 1947.

___. *Up Front*. New York: Henry Holt, 1947.

Noland, John. *The Rising Sun : the Decline and Fall of the Japanese Empire*. New York: Random House, 1970.

Pyle, Ernie. *Brave Men*. New York: Henry Holt, 1944.

Ryan, Cornelius. *The Longest Day, June 6, 1944*. New York: Simon and Schuster, 1959.

Sajer, Guy. *The Forgotten Soldier, Memoirs of a German Soldier*. New York: Harper & Row, 1971.

Sandler, Stanley. *Segregated Skies: All Black Combat Squadrons of World War II*. Blue Ridge Summit, Pennsylvania: Smithsonian Institution Press, 1992.

Snyder, Louis. *Encyclopedia of the Third Reich*. New York: Paragon, 1989.

Terkel, Studs. *The Good War*. New York: Ballantine, 1984.

Toland, John. *Story of the Bulge*. New York: Random House, 1959.

___. *The Rising Sun: The Decline and Fall of the Japanese Empire*. New York: Random House, 1970.

Van der Vat, Dan. *The Pacific Campaign: The U.S.-Japanese Naval War*. n.p., Touchstone, 1992.

Weigley, Russell. *Eisenhower's Lieutenants*. Bloomington: University of Indiana, 1981.

White, W.L. *They Were Expendable* [Motor Torpedo Boats]. New York: Harcourt, Brace,1942.

Yahil, Leni. *The Holocaust*. New York: Oxford University, 1990.